YMPOLS OF THE

P9-AGP-783

DATE DUE

DE 2 1 02			
MY			

DEMCO 38-296

TRADEMARKS AND SYMBOLS OF THE WORLD

TRADEMARKS AND SYMBOLS OF THE WORLD

**BY
YUSAKU KAMEKURA
PREFACE BY
PAUL RAND**

REINHOLD PUBLISHING CORPORATION
New York

CONTENTS

5 : Preface by Paul Rand

8 : Foreword

11 : Illustrations

241 : Some Notes on Trademark Design

259 : Illustration Credits

285 : Index of Designers

288 : Index of Clients

Published in the United States of America
by Reinhold Publishing Corporation, New York, 1965
Printed and bound in Japan
by Zokeisha Publications Limited, Tokyo
All rights reserved
Library of Congress Catalog Card No. 65-24055

A few years ago, in an introduction to a collection of my own trademarks,
I wrote the following:

A trademark
is a picture.
It is a symbol
a sign
an emblem
an escutcheon
...an image.

There are
good symbols...
like the cross.
There are
others...
like the swastika.
Their meanings
are taken
from reality.

Symbols
are a duality.
They take on
meaning

from causes
...good or bad.
And they give
meaning
to causes
...good or bad.
The flag
is a symbol
of a country.
The cross
is a symbol
of a religion.
The swastika
was a symbol
of good luck
until
its meaning
was changed.

The vitality
of a symbol
comes

from effective
dissemination...
by the state
by the community
by the church
by the corporation.
It needs
attending
to get
attention.

The trademark
is a symbol
of a corporation.
It is not
a sign of
quality...
it is a sign of
the quality.
The trademark
for Chanel
smells

as good as
the perfume
it stands for.
This
is the blending
of form
and content.

Trademarks
are animate
inanimate
organic
geometric.
They are letters
ideograms
monograms
colors
things.
Ideally
they do not
illustrate
they indicate.

They are not
representational
but suggestive.

A trademark
is created
by a designer,
but *made*
by a corporation.
A trademark
is a picture,
an image...
the image
of a corporation.

In assembling his first book, *Trademarks of the World*, Mr. Kamekura focused our attention on the universality of the problem of identification and, happily, on the high level of imagination and skill that designers of many countries have brought to bear on this most important and difficult design assignment.

In this new book he goes one step further, showing us not only the trademarks but, more importantly, their application to a variety of practical problems. Not only do we gain insight into the designer's skills around the world; but, from Kamekura's selections for this volume, we learn something of the taste and viewpoint of a singular designer.

Weston, Connecticut 1965

Paul Rand

FOREWORD

When I wrote my previous book *Trademarks of the World* (New York, 1956), Bernard Rudofsky chided me by saying, "You must not bring out such a convenient book. It will only spoil designers by making it too easy for them." These words, coming from a man whose work I greatly admire, gave me much food for thought. Nevertheless, ten years later, I have prepared another "convenient" book.

After the previous work had gone through several printings, and I was on the point of letting it die a natural death, I received numerous requests for a revised edition incorporating additional material. After long deliberation, I finally decided that it would be better to prepare an entirely new book of the outstanding trademarks and symbols created during the last ten years. I was fortunate in receiving the greatest cooperation from outstanding designers throughout the world, who generously sent me samples of their work. I take this opportunity to thank them for their assistance which has made this book possible.

The reader who looks at this book, will not find anything "Japanese" about it, even though the author is a Japanese. However, I am firmly of the opinion that trademarks, symbols, and signs must speak an international language.

This book contains 763 entries selected from about 2,000 items received. I have tried to express my own attitudes in the way the entries are arranged, and in the rhythm that this has created.

I have no intention of providing a long text. I hope that the selection and arrangement of the items included, and the rhythm they carry, are themselves a visual essay in an international language.

As he did for my previous book, Paul Rand was good enough to contribute a splendid preface, for which I am deeply grateful. I am indeed proud to be able to call this great artist my friend.

I would also like to thank Miss Yumiko Onishi for her assistance throughout the entire lengthy process of compiling this book.

Tokyo, April 1965

Yusaku Kamekura

2

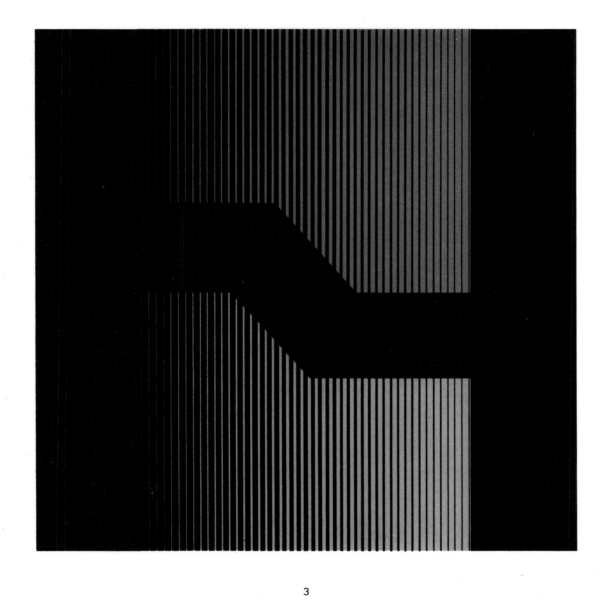

3

4

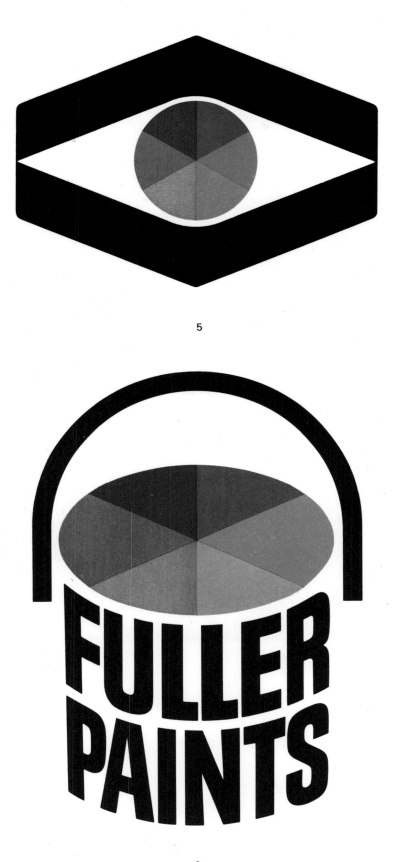

5

FULLER
PAINTS

6

7

8

9

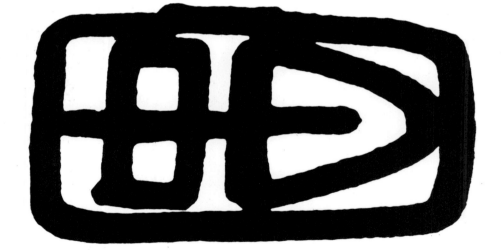

10

LIGHTCRAFT

11

12

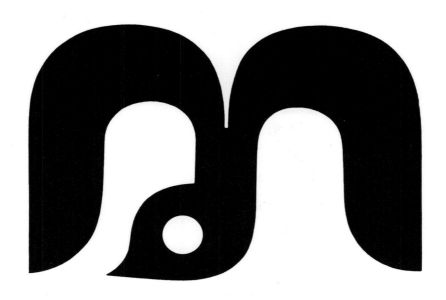

13

14

IBM

IBM

16

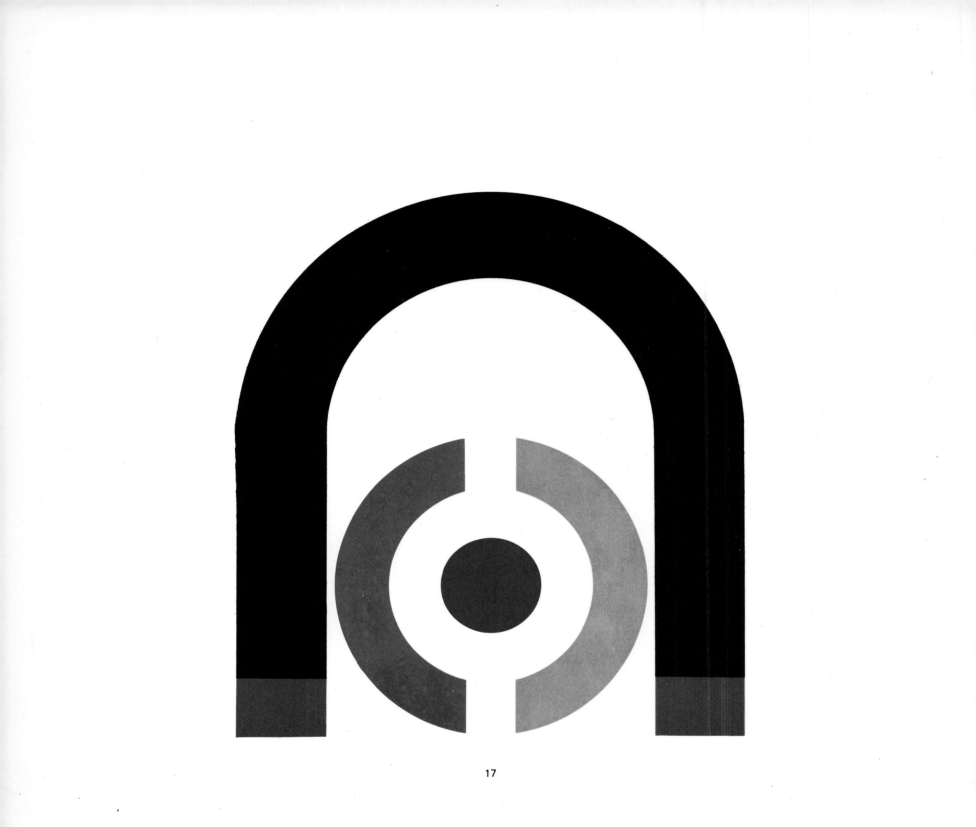

17

18

19

20

21

22

23

24

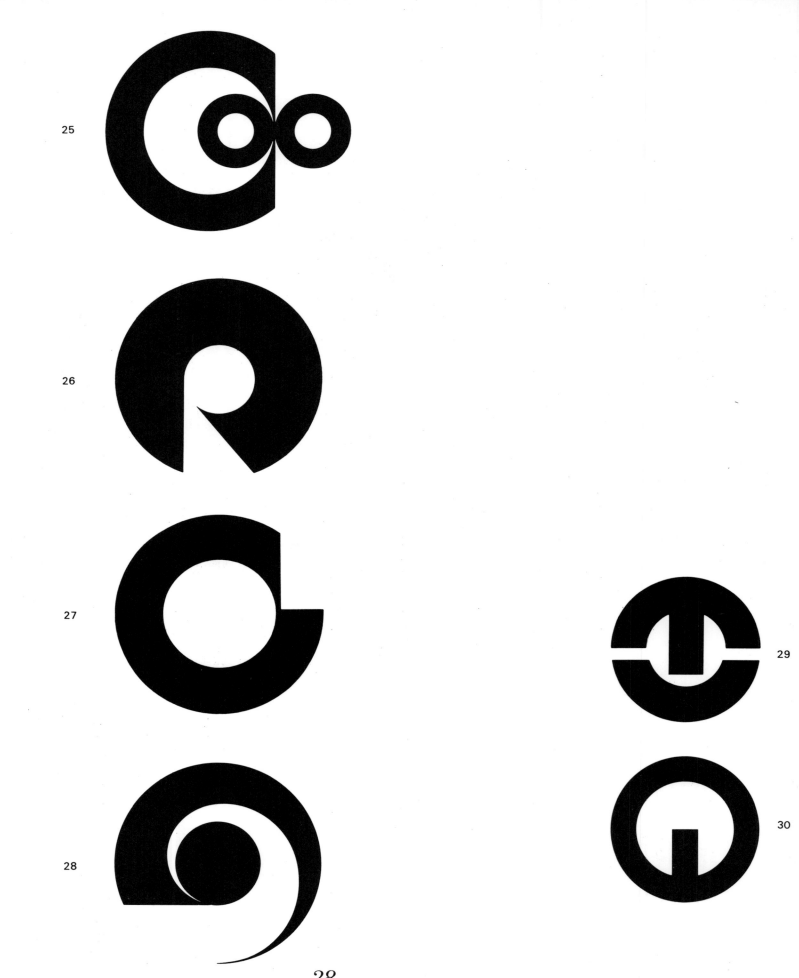

33

31

32

35

36

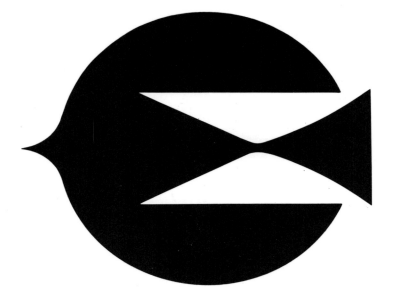

37

38

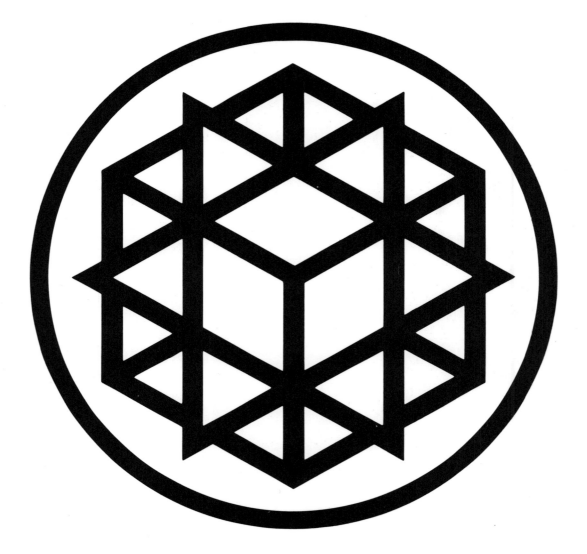

40

41

42

43

45

46

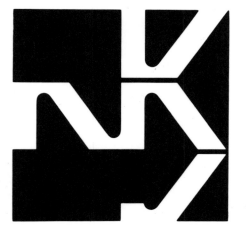

44

47

48

49

50

51

52

53

54

p

colo
_ol

LIGNOPLAST

gromalto

59

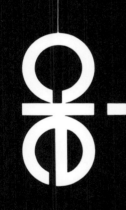

60

61

buri

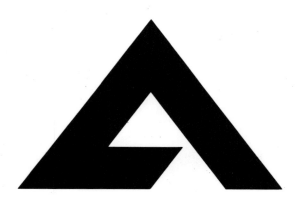

62

63

64

65

66

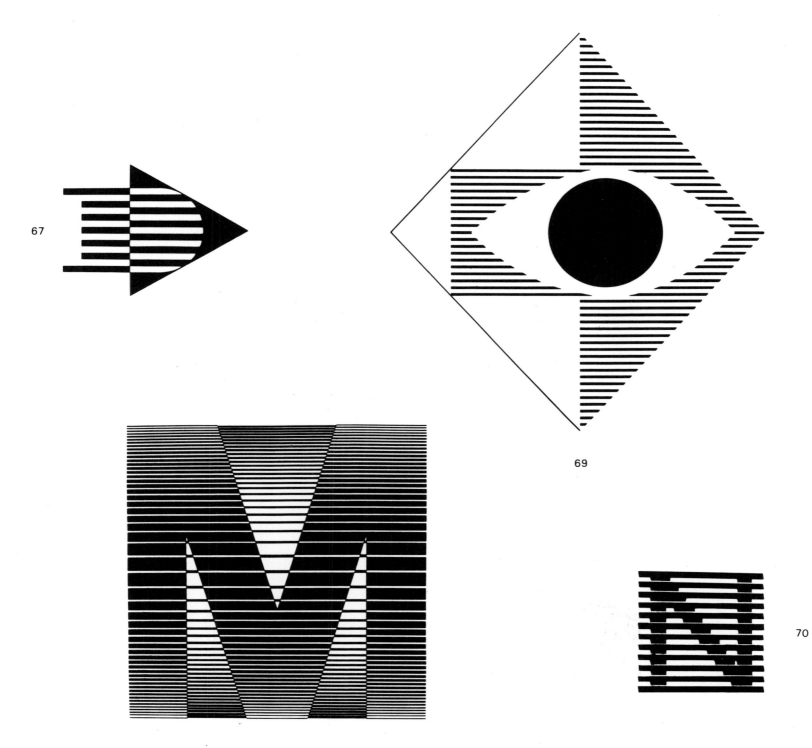

67

69

68

70

71

72

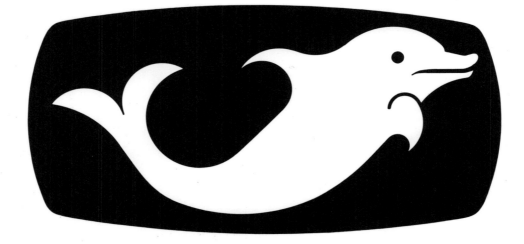

73

74

75

76

78

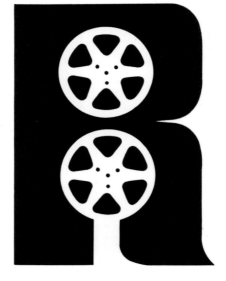

77

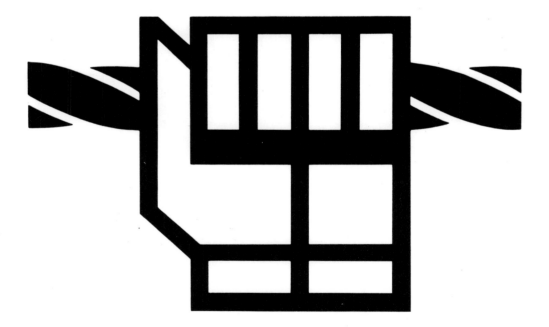

81

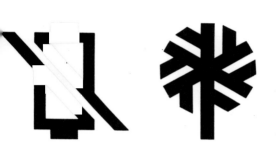

79   80

82

83

84

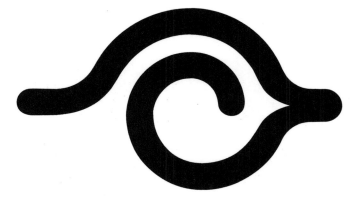

85

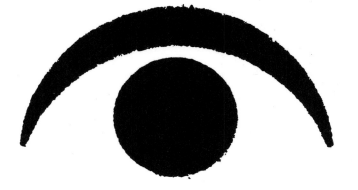

87

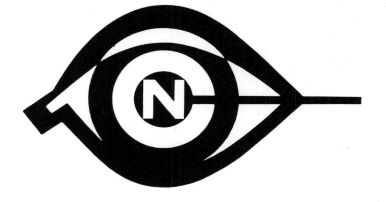

86

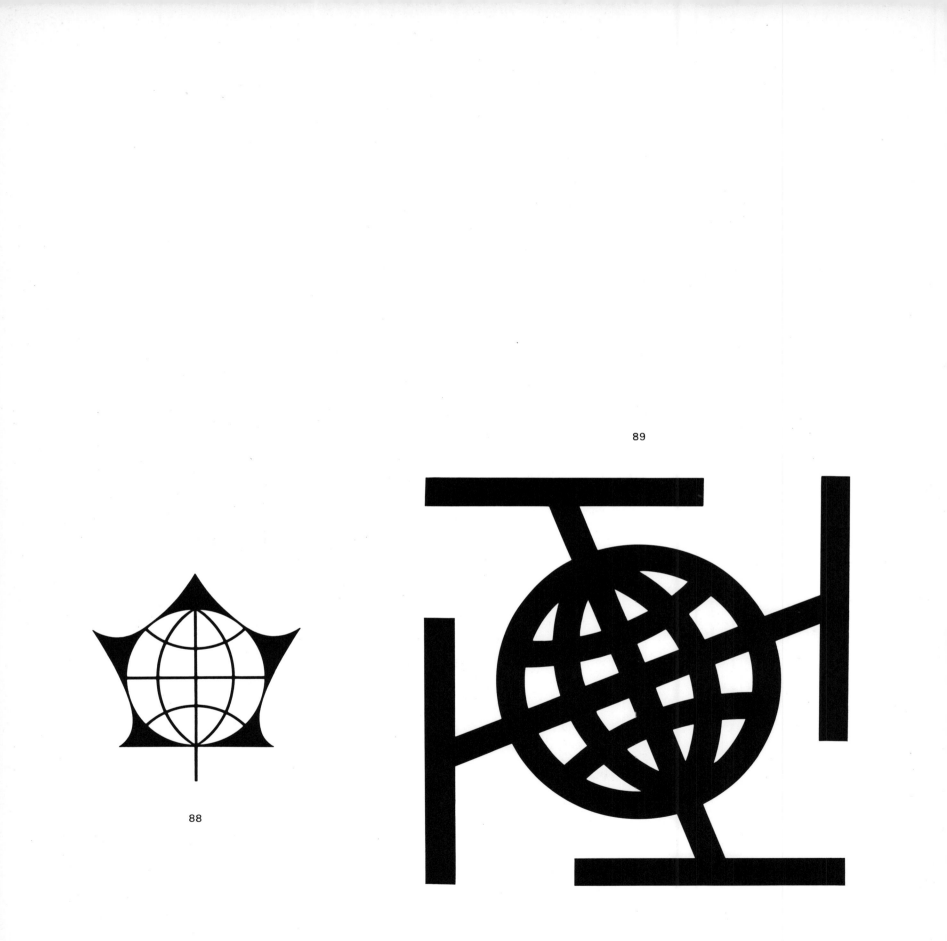

88

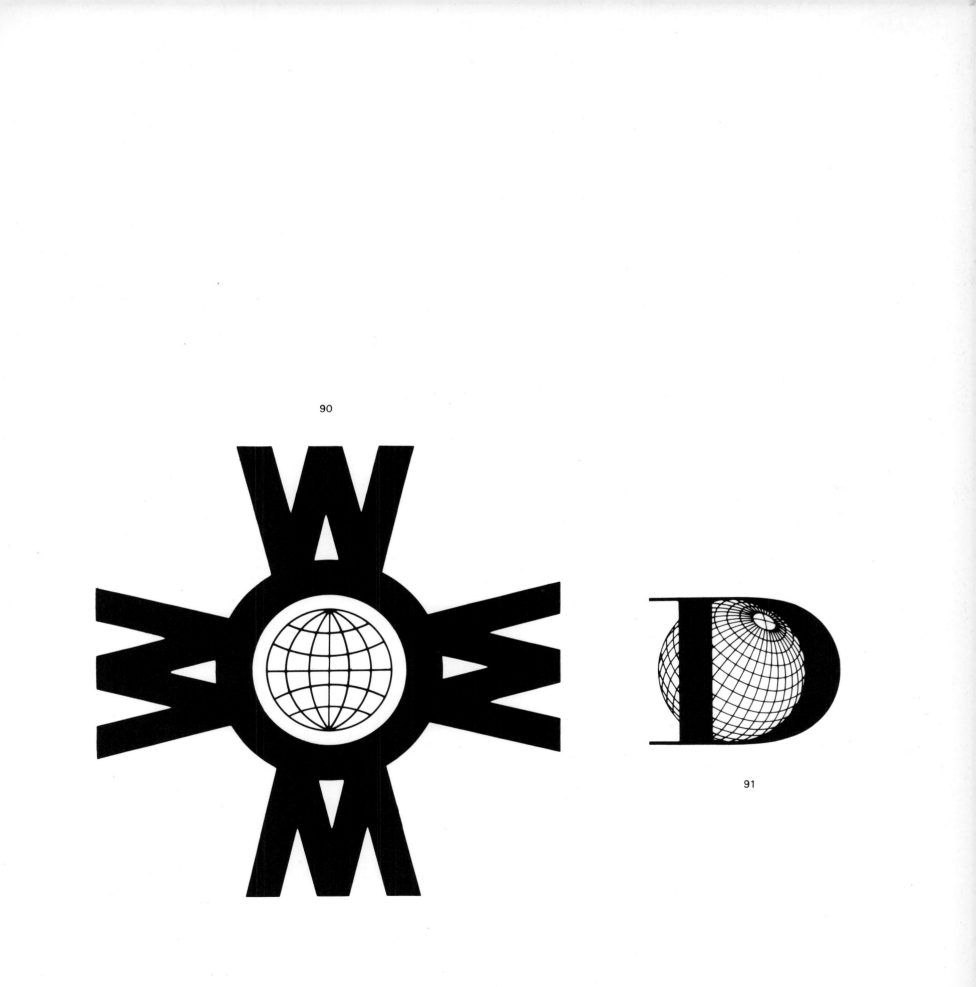

91

92

93

95

96

97

98

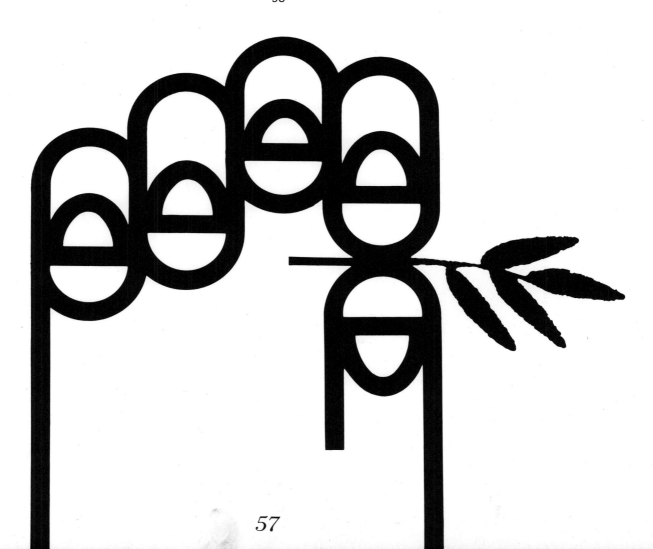

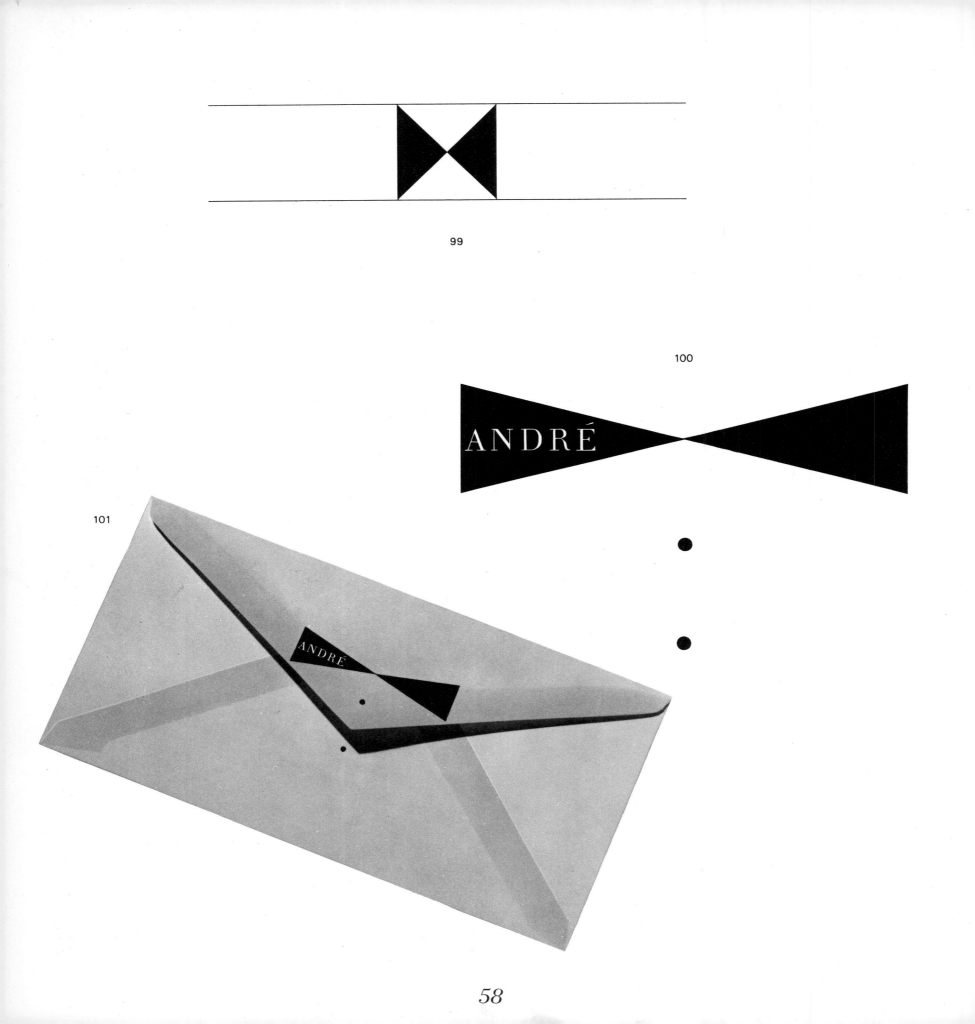

99

100

ANDRÉ

101

102

103

104

Papyrus AG

105

106

Herb
Lubalin
223 E· 31 St·
New York
10016
Or 9·2636·7

108

109

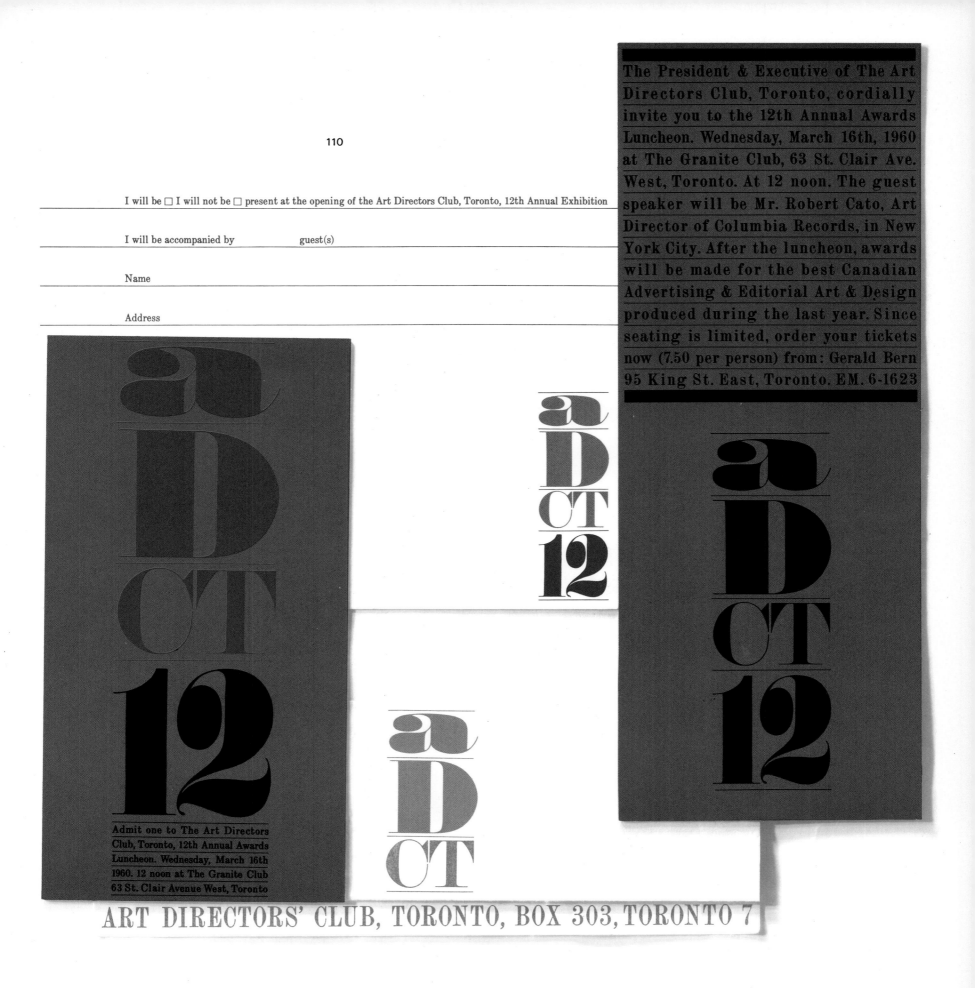

110

I will be ☐ I will not be ☐ present at the opening of the Art Directors Club, Toronto, 12th Annual Exhibition

I will be accompanied by   guest(s)

Name

Address

The President & Executive of The Art Directors Club, Toronto, cordially invite you to the 12th Annual Awards Luncheon. Wednesday, March 16th, 1960 at The Granite Club, 63 St. Clair Ave. West, Toronto. At 12 noon. The guest speaker will be Mr. Robert Cato, Art Director of Columbia Records, in New York City. After the luncheon, awards will be made for the best Canadian Advertising & Editorial Art & Design produced during the last year. Since seating is limited, order your tickets now (7.50 per person) from: Gerald Bern 95 King St. East, Toronto. EM. 6-1623

Admit one to The Art Directors Club, Toronto, 12th Annual Awards Luncheon. Wednesday, March 16th 1960. 12 noon at The Granite Club 63 St. Clair Avenue West, Toronto

ART DIRECTORS' CLUB, TORONTO, BOX 303, TORONTO 7

111

112

113

114

alluminio

115

riri

116

therma

117

118

119

120

121

122

124

123

125

126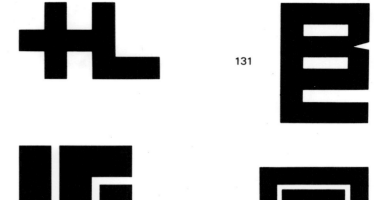

131

127

132

128

133

129

134

135

130

136

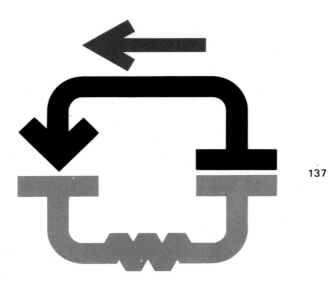

137

138

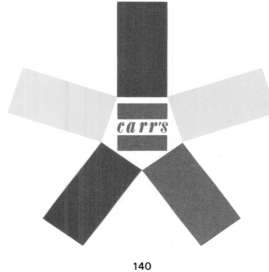

140

139

Essex Green Shopping Plaza — West Orange, New Jersey

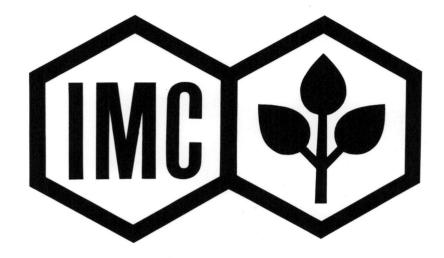

143

144

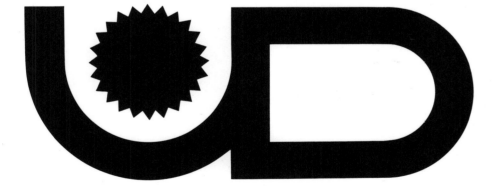

145

146

148

147

149

150

151

152

153

spinner.

155

154

156

157

MONO

miwa

158

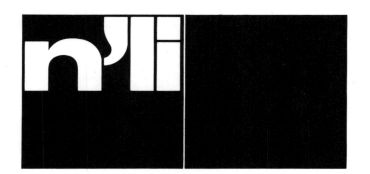

159

160

161

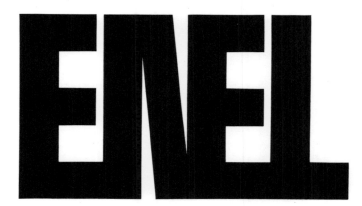

162

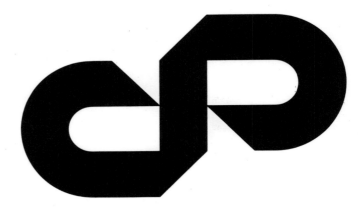

164

165

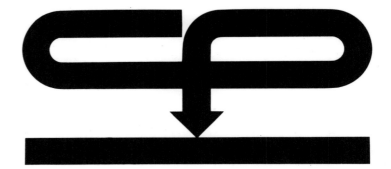

166

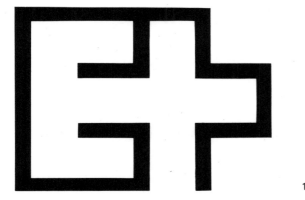

163

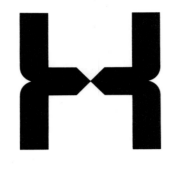

167

168

169

170

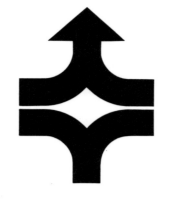

171

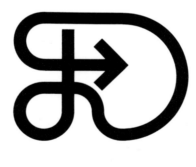

172

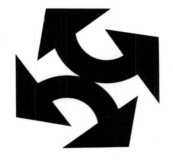

173

174

175

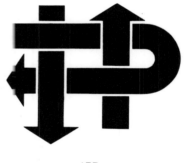

176

177

178

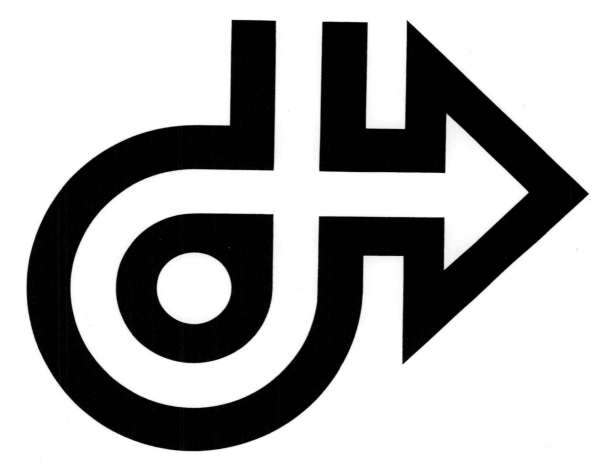

179

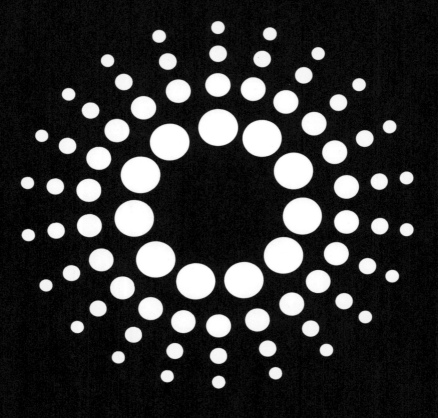

180

181

182

183

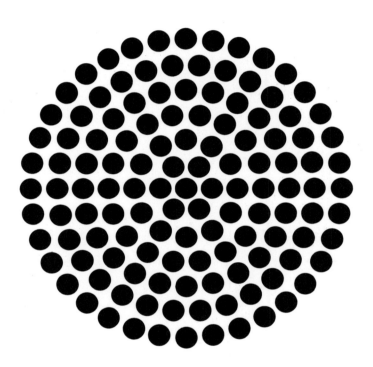

184

185

186

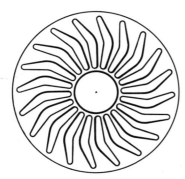

187   188

189   190

191   192

193   194

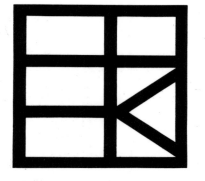
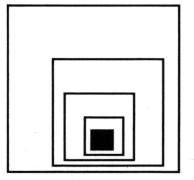

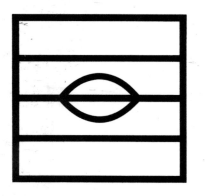
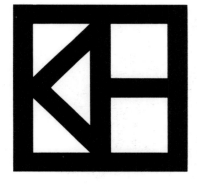

198

199

200

201

202

203

204

205

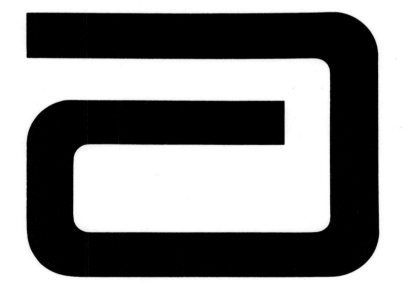

206

207

208

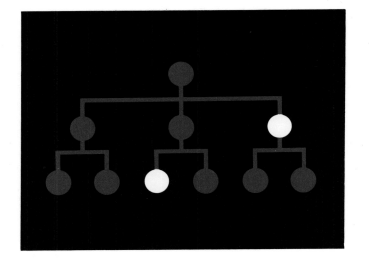

209

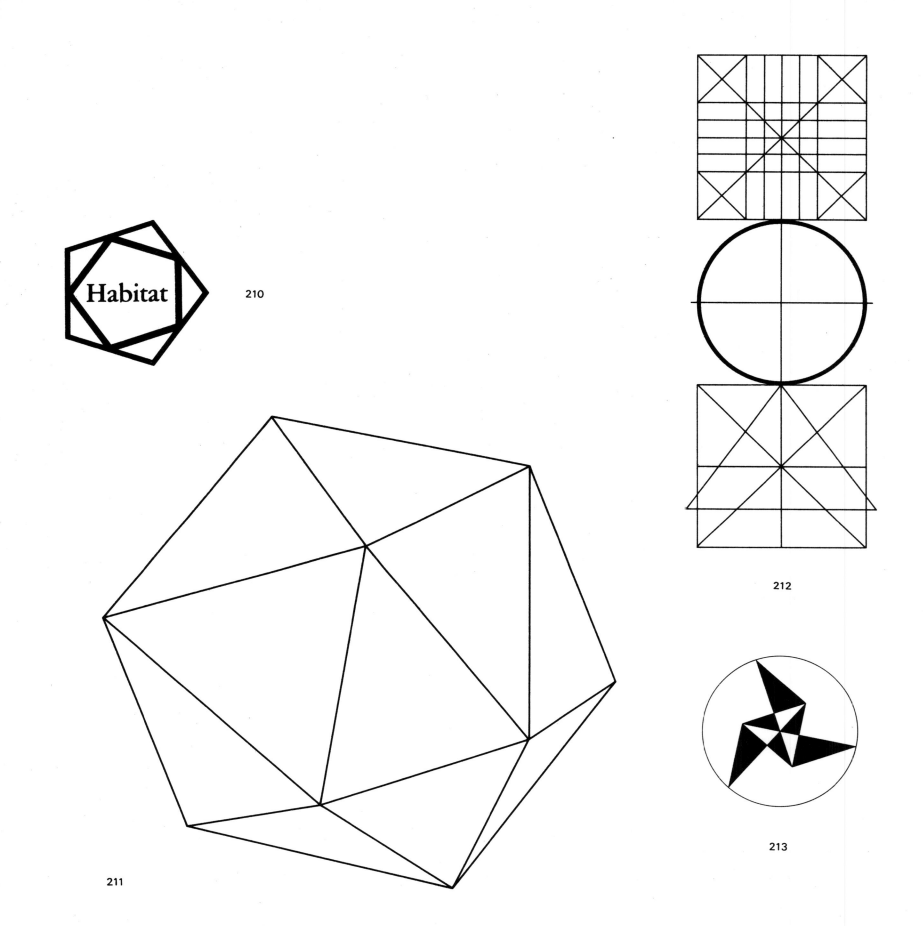

210

Habitat

211

212

213

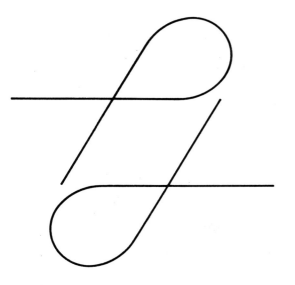

214

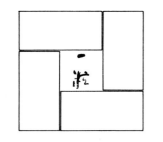

215

216

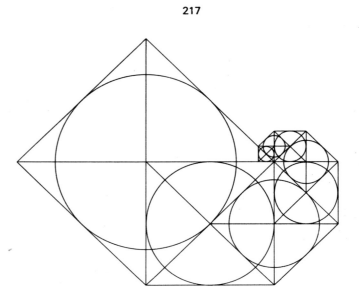

217

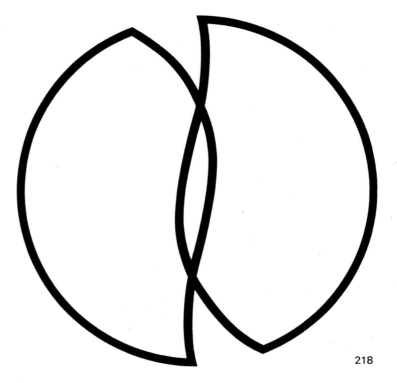

218

EROS

219

220

221

222

HARRIDGE'S

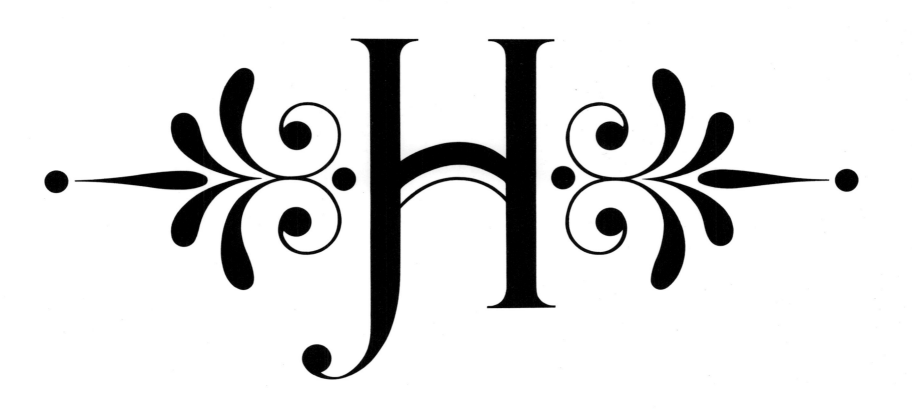

223

224

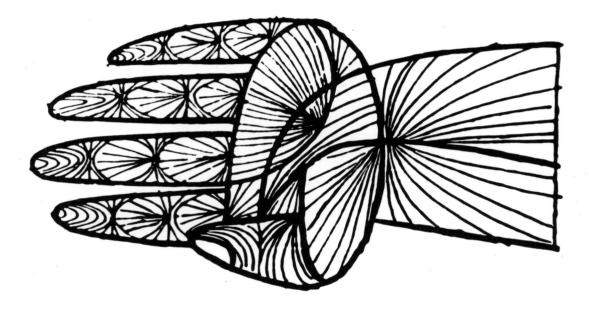

225

227

228

229

230

231

232

233

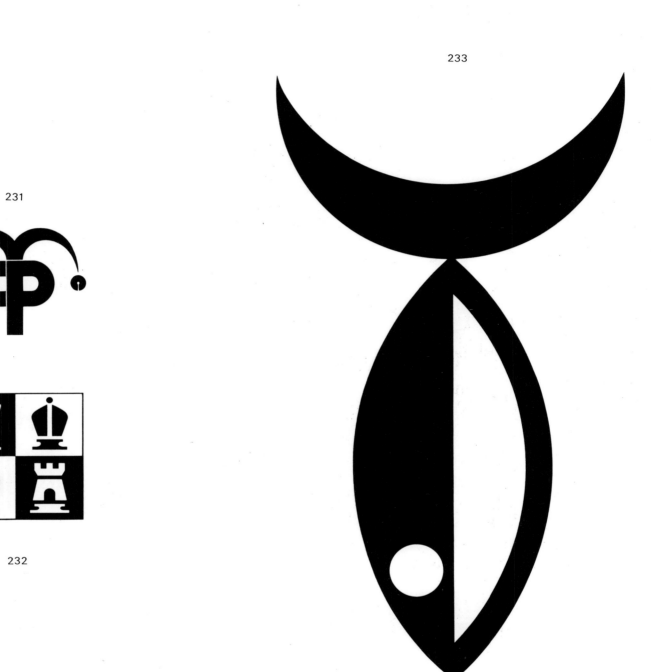

234

235

THEWHISKYHOUSE

236

237

WATNEYS

238

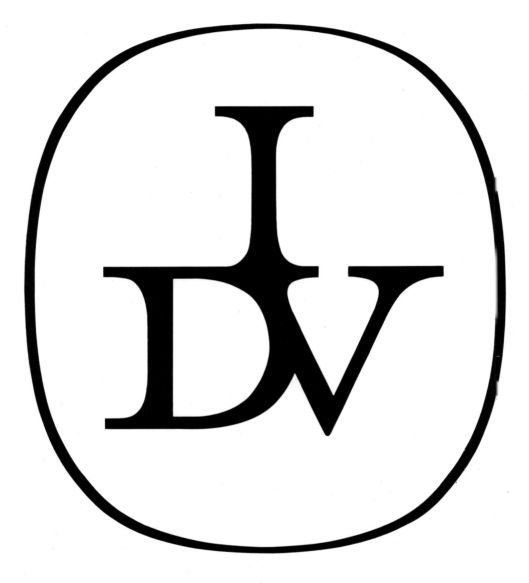

239

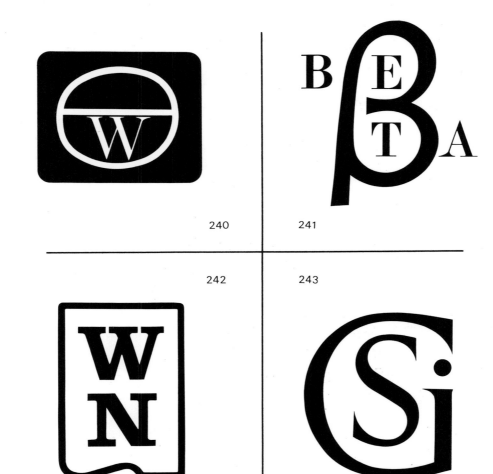

240

241

242

243

244

245

246

247

248

249 250

251 252

253 254

255

256

257

259

258

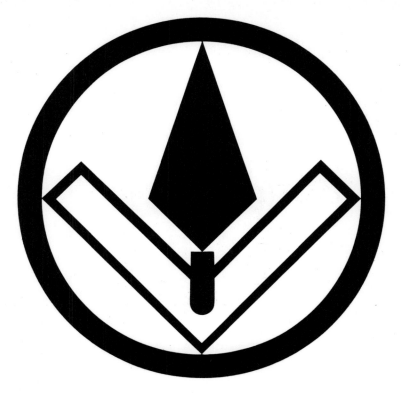

260

261

262

ARTEMIS
BÜCHER
BEFLÜGELN

264

265

266

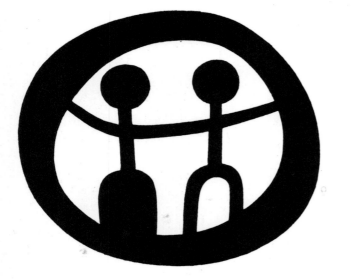

CASHMERE BOUQUET

PRESS

DO NOT
DISTURB

NAME
ROOM NO.
PLEASE FILL OUT LAUNDRY SLIP FOUND IN
DESK DRAWER AND PLACE INSIDE LAUNDRY BAG

THE NEW YORK | HILTON
at | Rockefeller Center

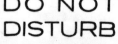

LAWRY'S

268

_____

269

titeflex

270

274

271

272

273

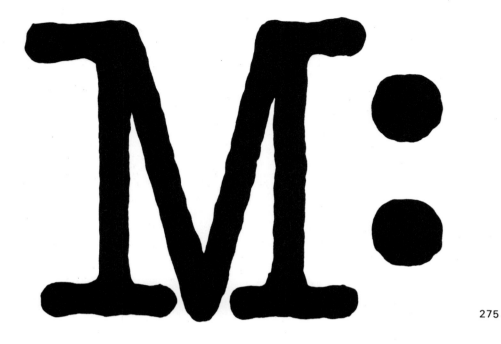

275

276

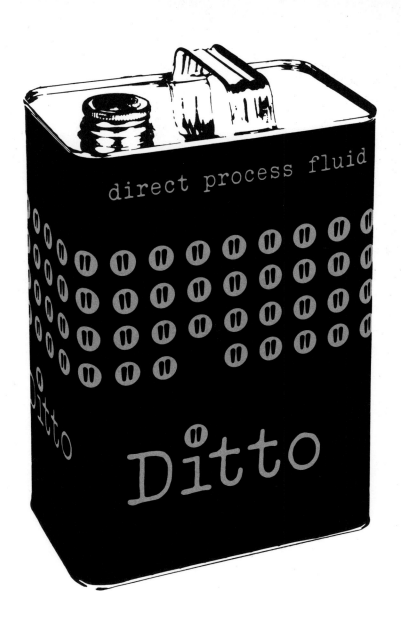

277

278

279

281

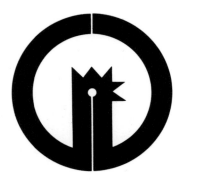

285

283

286

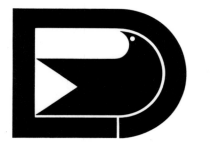

284

287

288

293

289

294

290

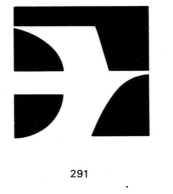

291

292

T

THE TRANE COMPANY

Ivan Allen Co.
29 Pryor St., N. E. Atlanta 3, Georgia JAckson 1-0800

G
B
R

E·N·I

Erik Nitsche International S. A. rue Voltaire 8 Genève, Suisse

Samsonite Luggage Division

Shwayder Brothers Incorporated
1050 South Broadway
Denver 17, Colorado
Phone: SHerman 4-1701
Also manufacturers of
Samsonite Card Tables & Chairs
Detroit 29, Michigan

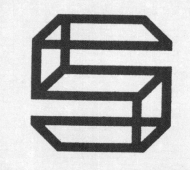

International

Golf

Association, inc.

John Jay Hopkins, Founder

American Design Foundation   160 East 56 Street   New York 22, N. Y.   PLaza 1-3350

Design Built Exhibits, Inc.  35-01 Vernon Blvd., Long Island City

303

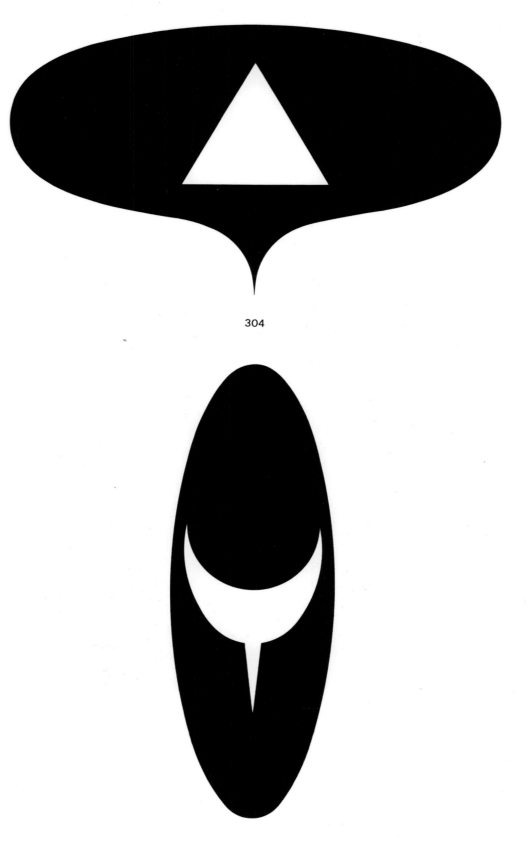

304

305

306

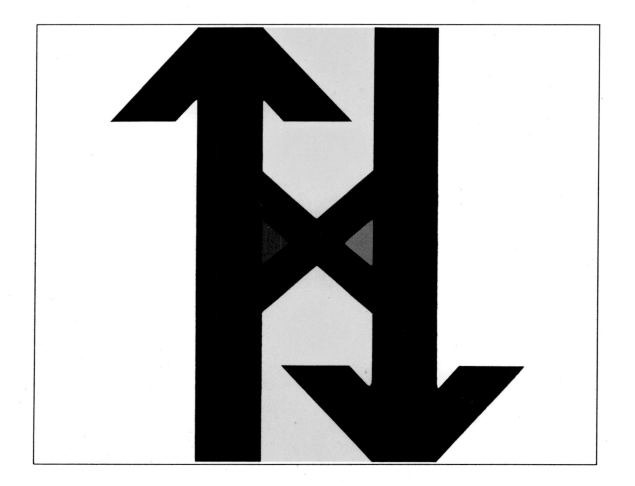

307

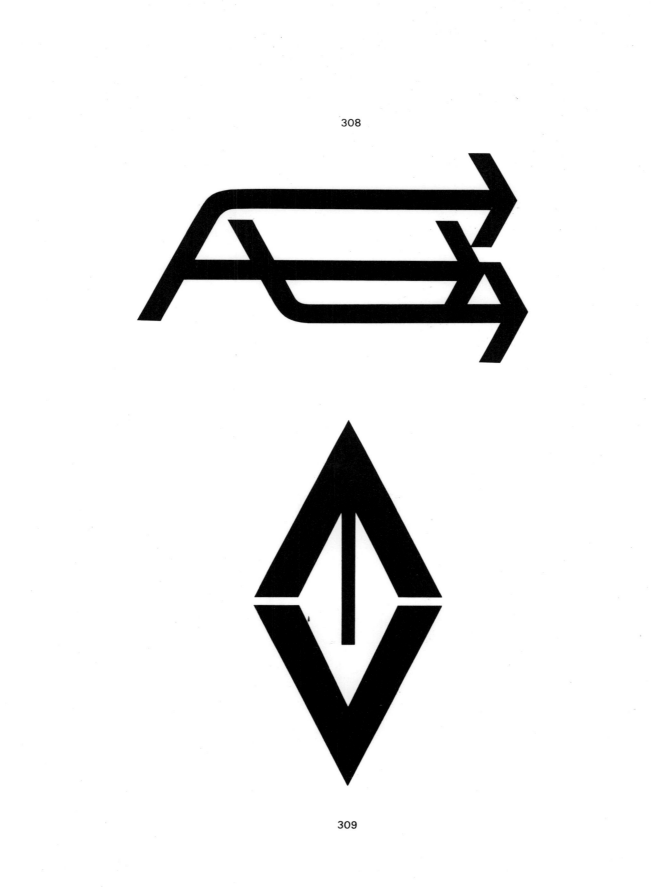

311

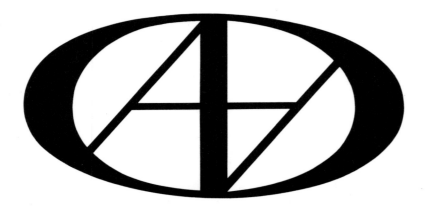

312

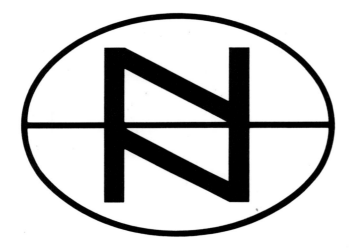

313

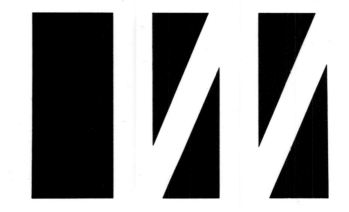

315

314

316

317

318

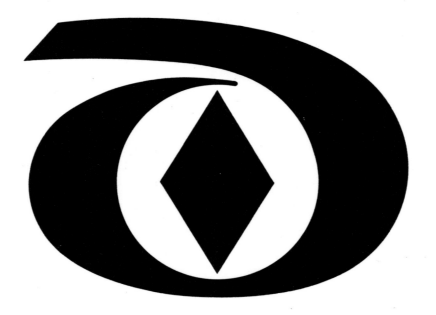

319

320

321

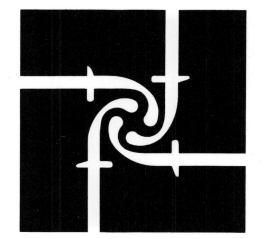

322

323

324

327

330

325

328

326

329

332

333

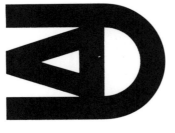

334

331

335

336

337

339

341

343

338

340

342

344

349

347

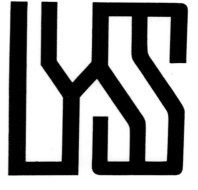

345

348

350

346

351

352

353

354

355

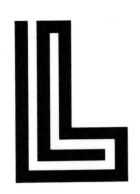

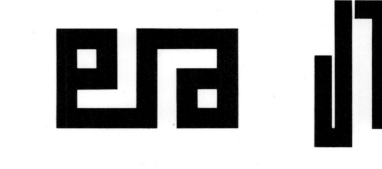

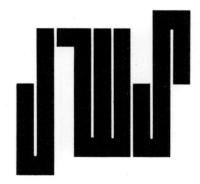

356

357

358

359

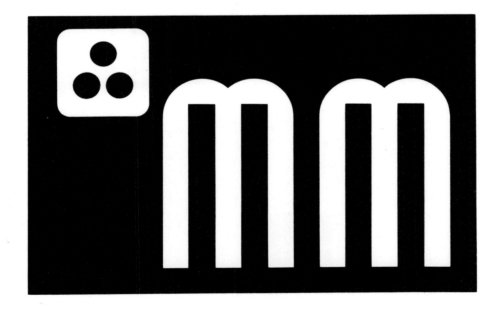

360

361

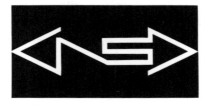

364

367

GALVANITE

362

368

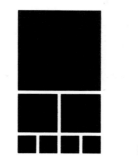

365

363

366

scei

369

370

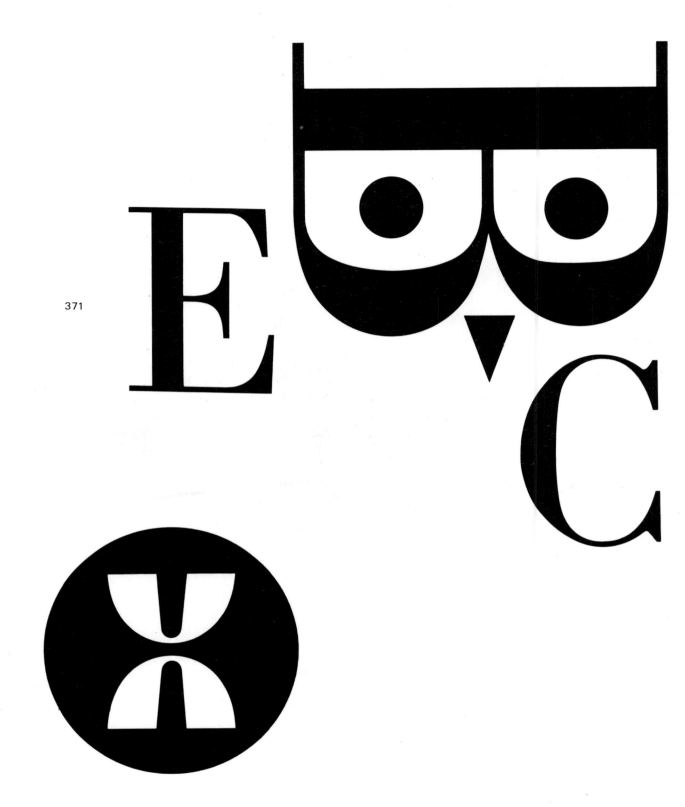

371

372

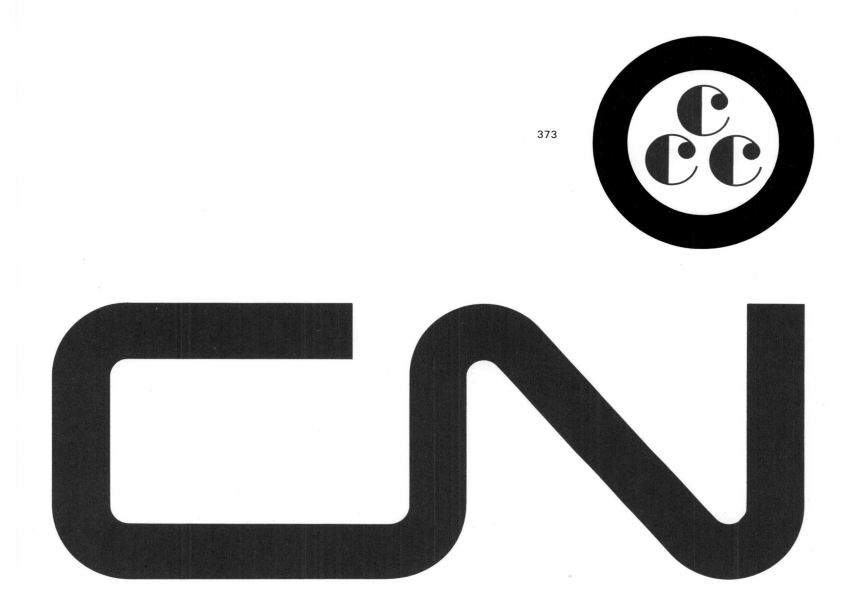

374

375

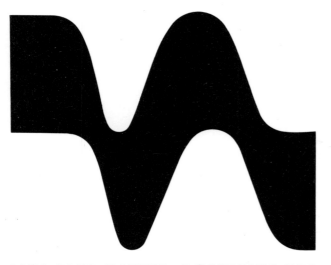

NOLAND PAPER COMPANY, INC.

376

377

378

379

380

JULIE'S

381

382

383

384

385

391

386

389

392

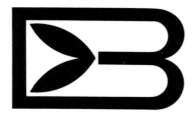

387

393

388

390

394

397

401

398

395

399

402

396

400

403

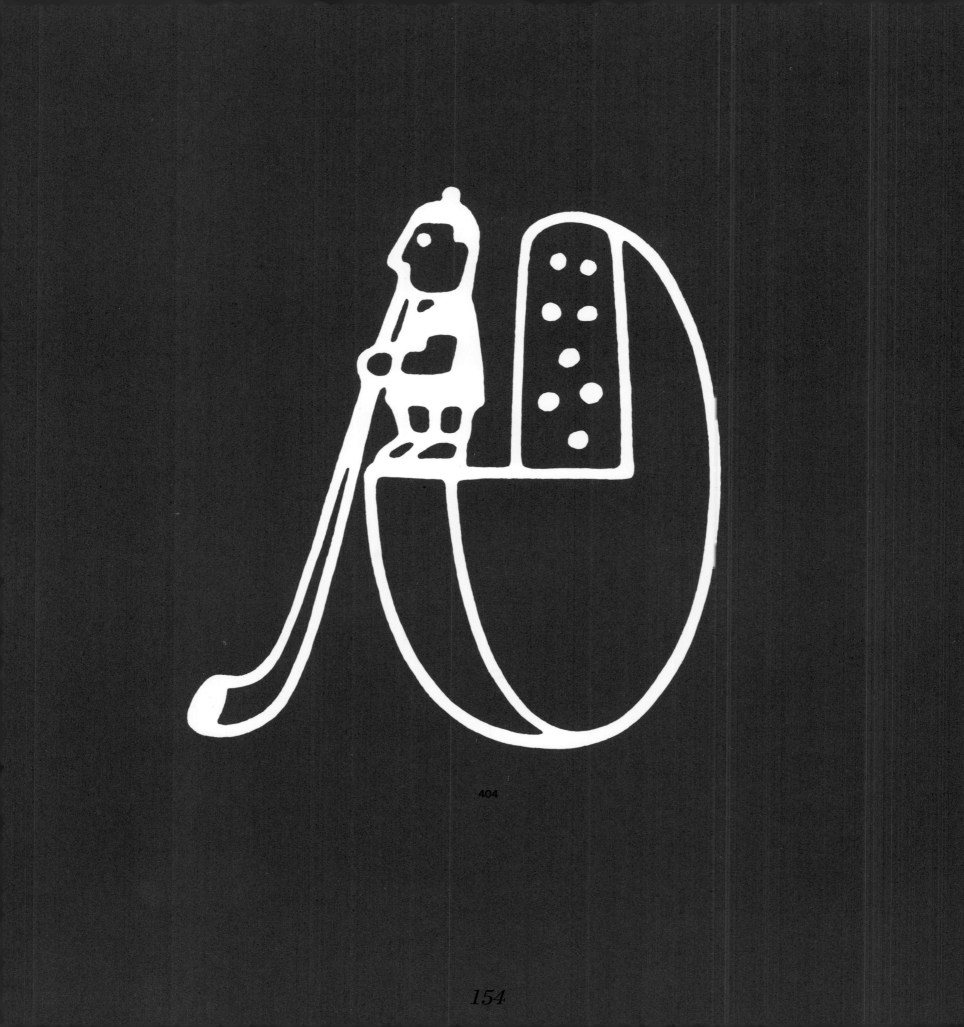

404

405

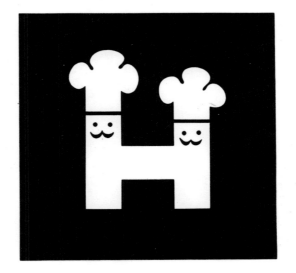

406

407

408

409

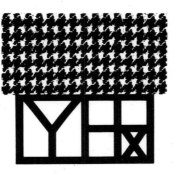

410

411

412

413

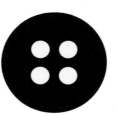

414

415

416

417

418

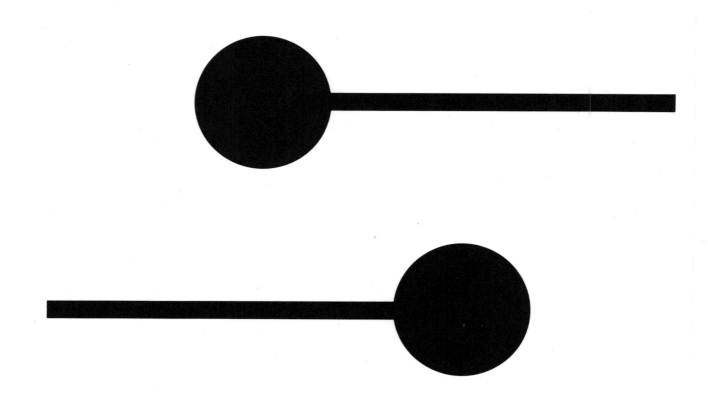

419

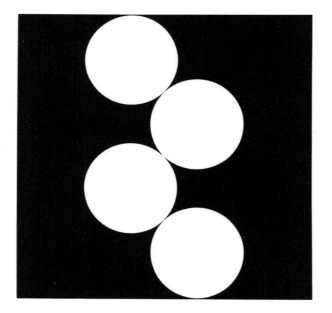

420

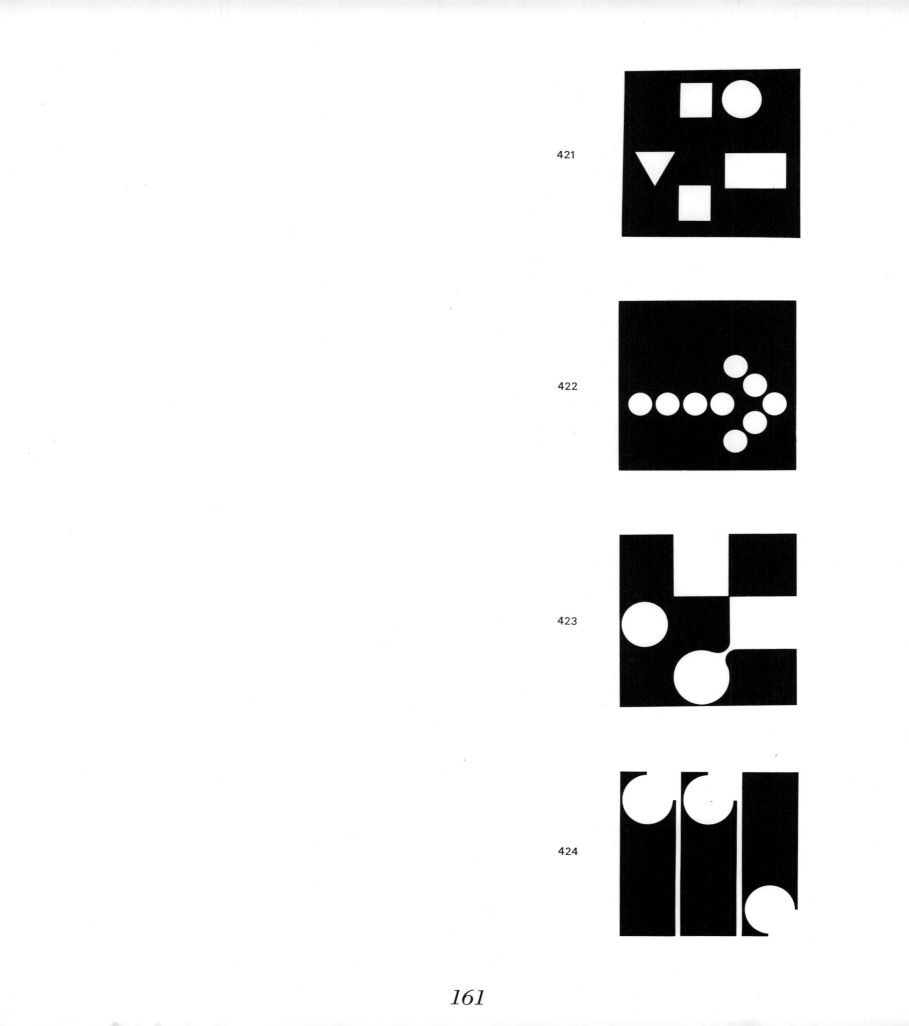

421

422

423

424

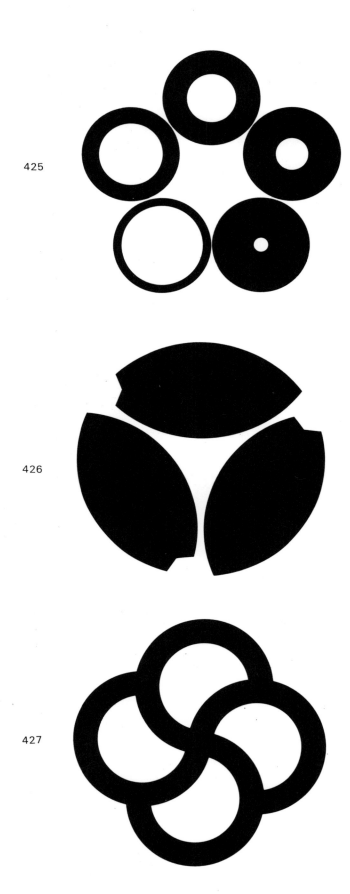

425

426

427

428

429

430

431

434

437

432

435

438

440

433

436

439

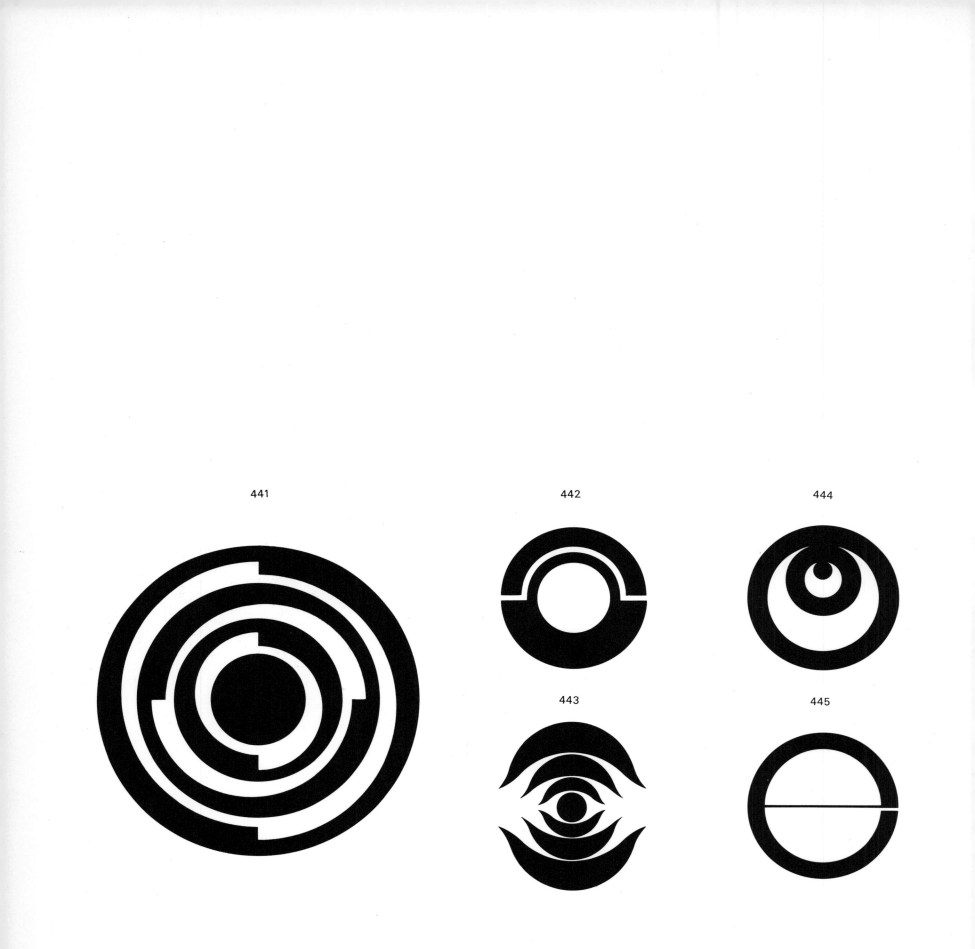

441

442

444

443

445

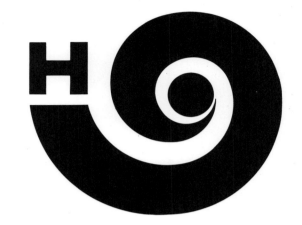

450

446

448

447

449

451

452

454

453

455

456

458

457

459

EQUITABLE

460

461

THE *LARK* BY STUDEBAKER

sangiorgio

462

463

SB&H SALOMON BROTHERS & HUTZLER

464

465

466 **ESTON**

chairmasters

467

Packaging 468

SYMPHONIE

469

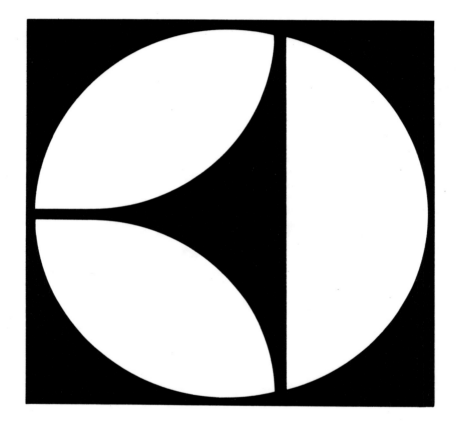

470

471

472

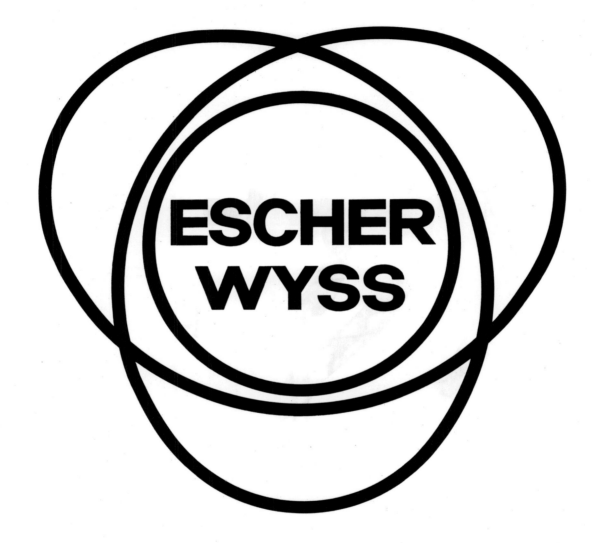

473

474

475

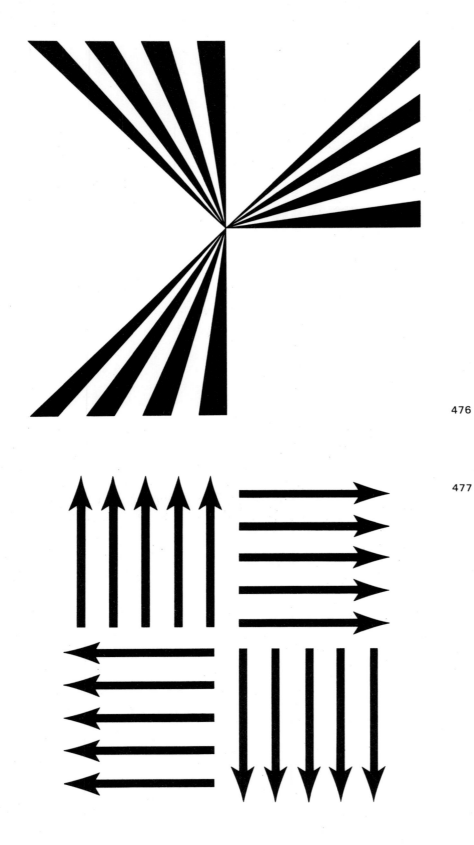

476

477

478

479

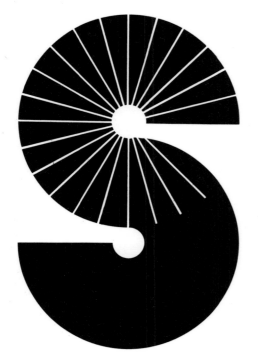

480

481

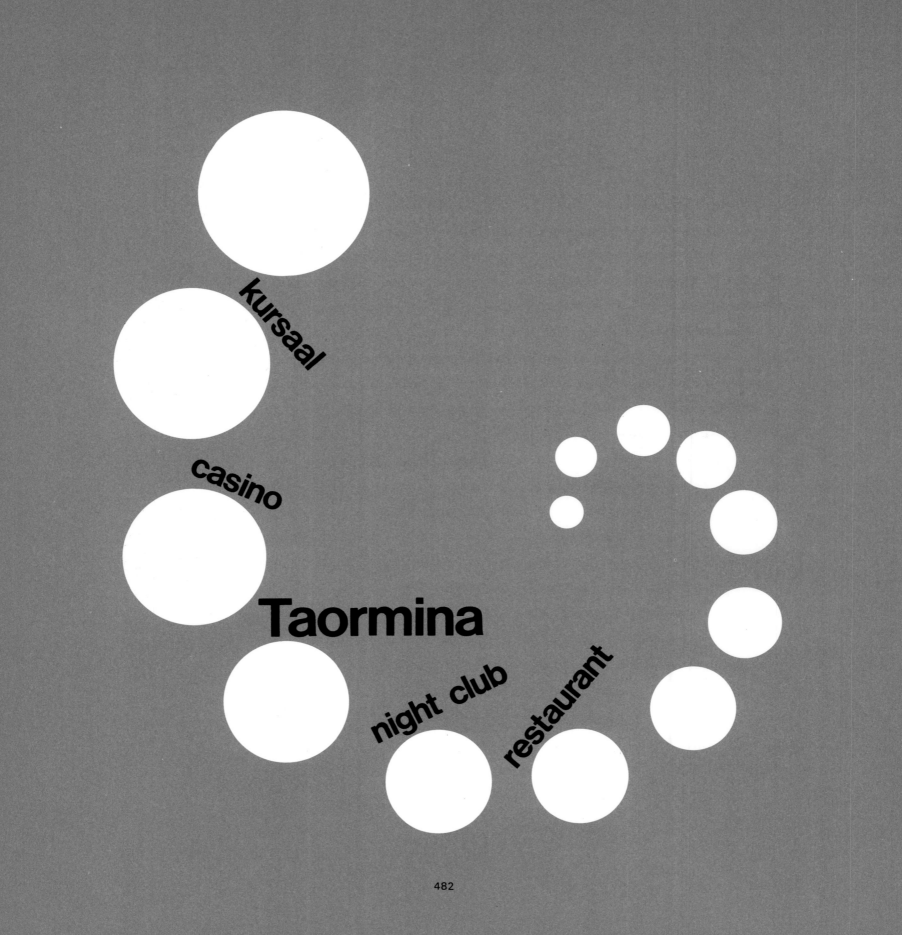

kursaal

casino

Taormina

night club

restaurant

482

483

484

485

486

487

488

489

490

496

491

492

493

494

495

497

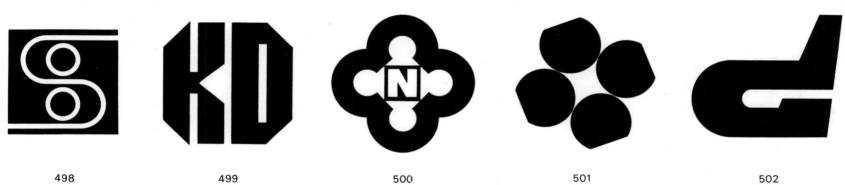

498   499   500   501   502

503   504   505   506   507

513

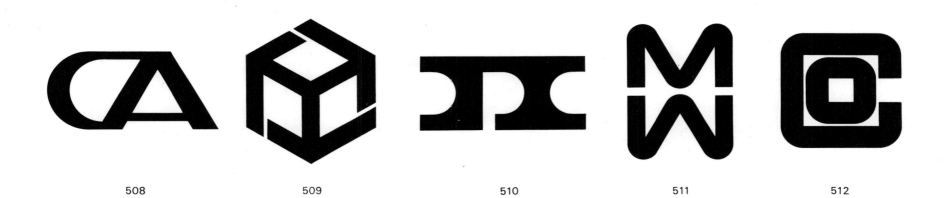

508 509 510 511 512

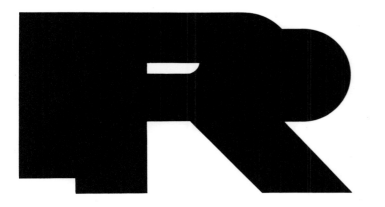

514

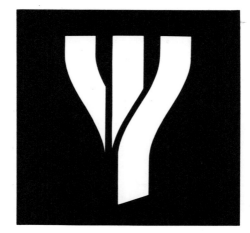

516

515

517

519

518

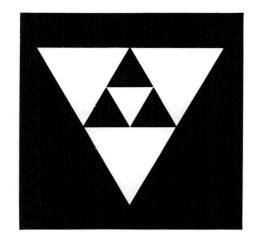

521

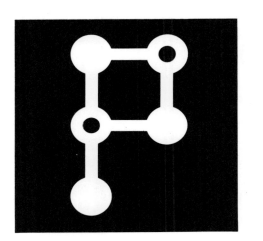

520

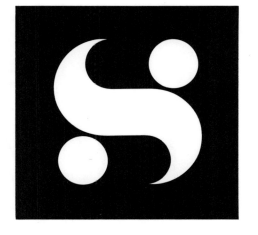

522

524

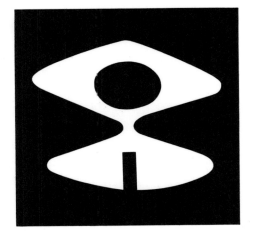

523

525

526

527

528

529

530

531

532

533

534

535

536

537

538

539

540

541

542

543

544

545

546

547

548

549

550

551

552

553

554

555

556

557

558

magnum

559

561

560

Westinghouse

562

563

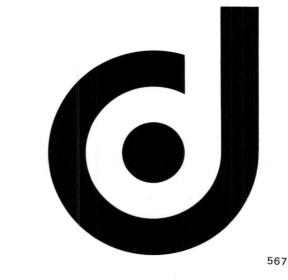

564

565

566

567

568

569

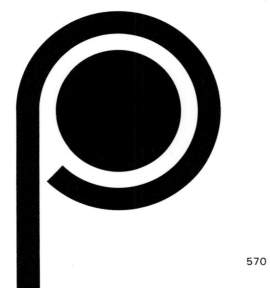

570

571

572

574

573

575

576

577

580 ——— 585

578

579

586

587

588

589

590

591

Rizzi

TELEFONO 22456   BORDIGHERA
VIA VITTORIO EMANUELE 251

592

FORNASETTI ORIGINALS

596

INTARSIO

597

CITTÀ DI CARTE

593

TIRO A SEGNO

594

BUONI BOCCONI

598

MEDAGLIONI
NELL'OTTAGONO

595

Sirene

FORNASETTI · MILANO
MADE IN ITALY

599

CANI
600

TEMA E
VARIAZIONI
604

ASTROLABIO
605

FORNASETTI MILANO
MADE IN ITALY
601

IL MONDO
ALLA ROVESCIA
606

SCULTORI
ITALIANI
602

STOVIGLIE
FORNASETTI
MILANO
MADE IN ITALY
1955
607

ASSI
603

FORNASETTI
MILANO-VIA MANZONI 17-TEL. 860004
608

609

610

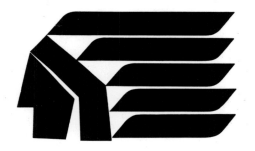

611

612

201

613

614

615

616

617

618

619

620

621

622

623

624

625

626

627

628

629

630

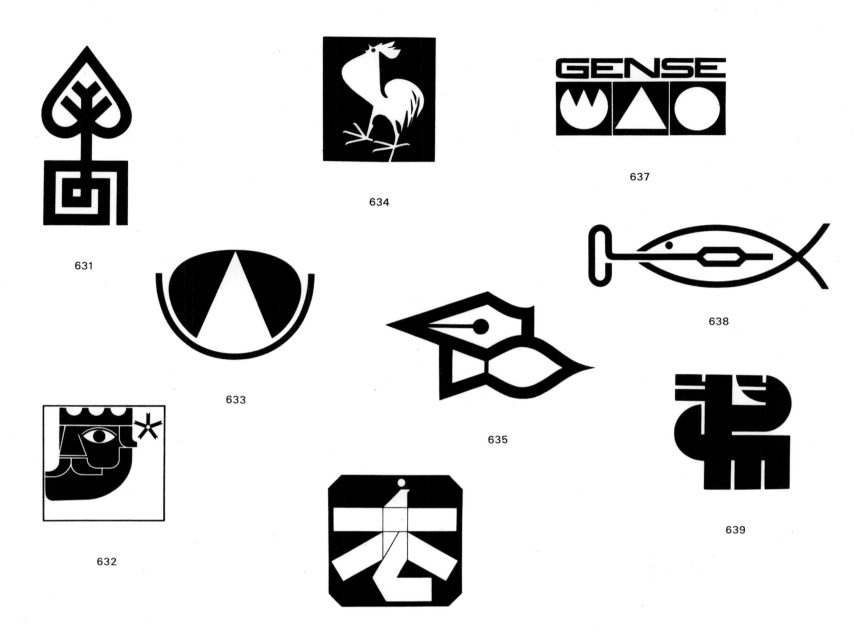

631

632

633

634

635

636

637

638

639

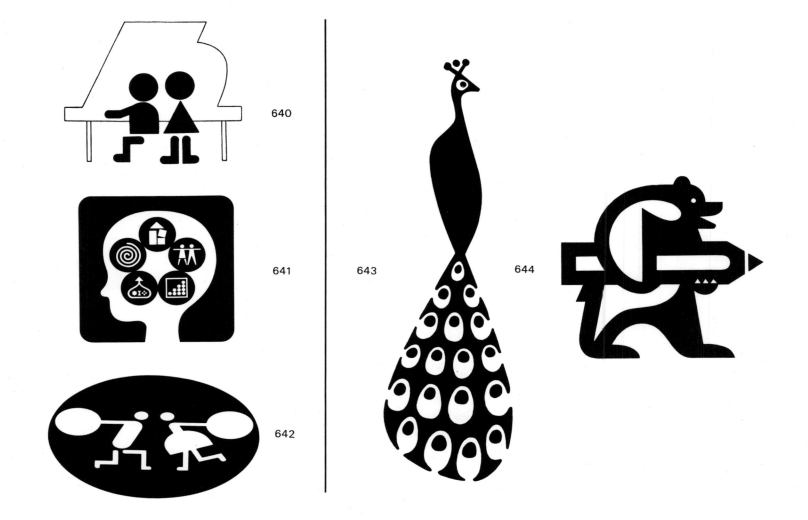

640

641

643

644

642

JUBILÆUMS KONGRESS

SSO

1961

BASEL

645

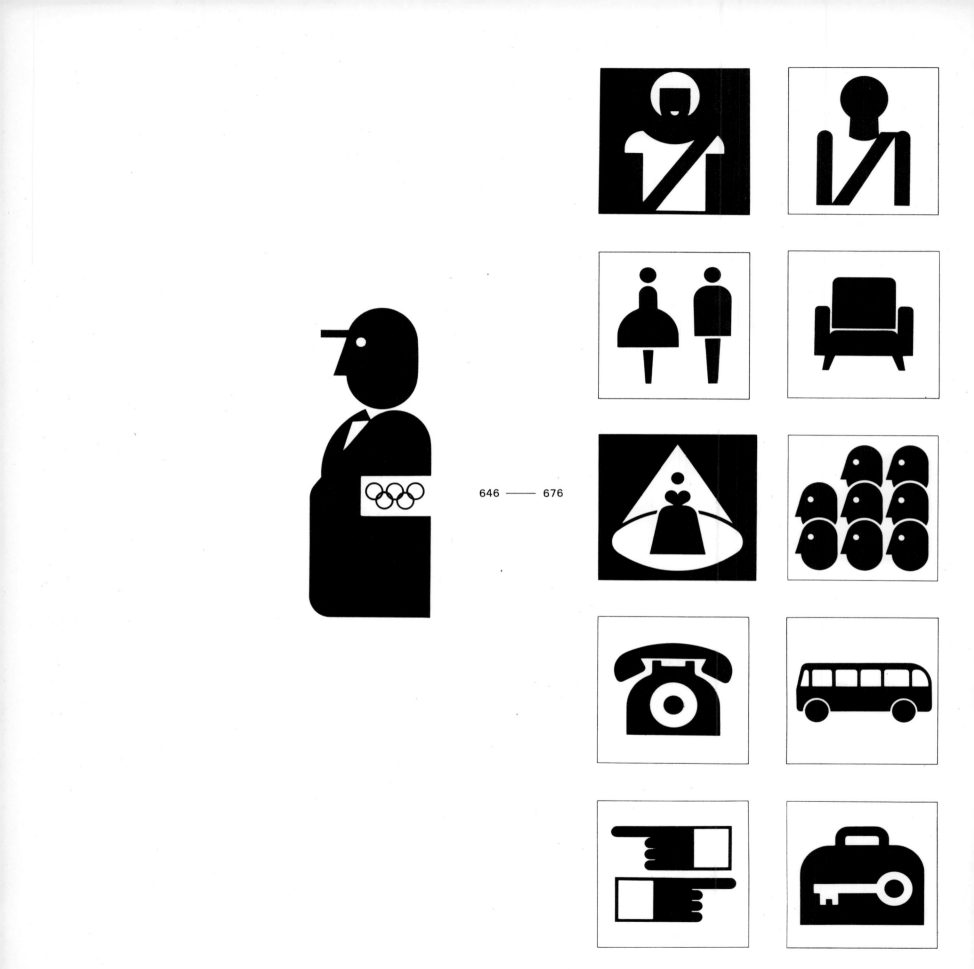

646 —— 676

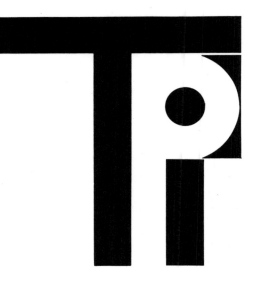

677

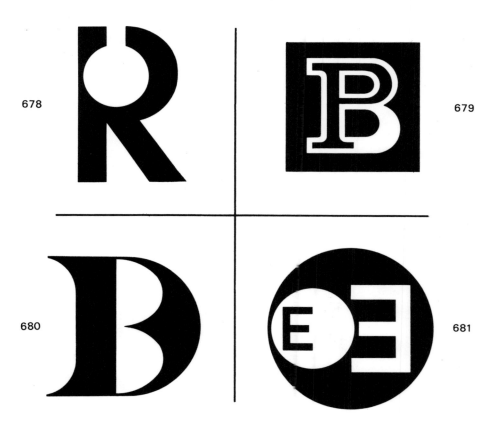

678

679

680

681

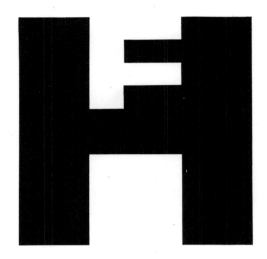

682

683

684

685

686

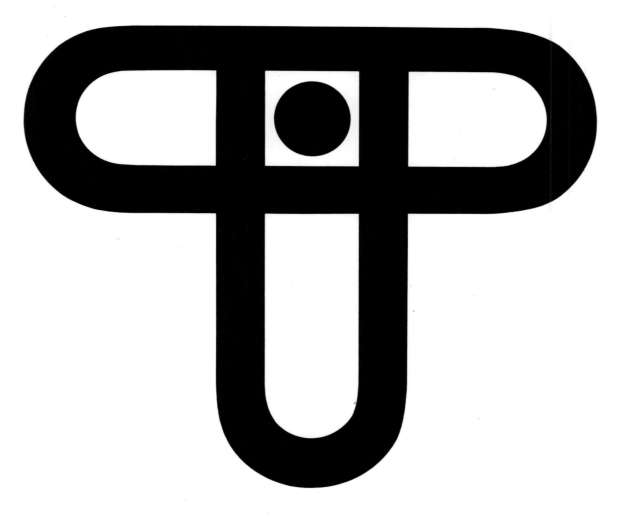

687

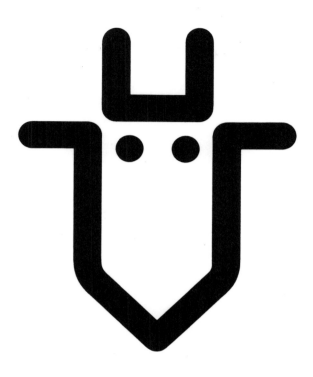

688

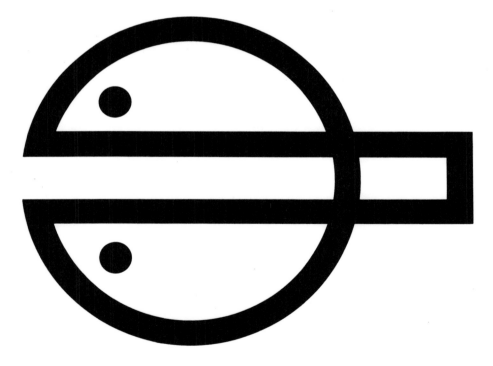

689

690

691

692

693

negi

694

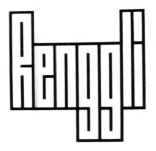

696

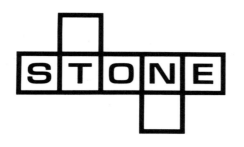

697

698

218

699

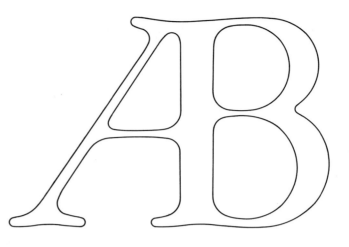

700

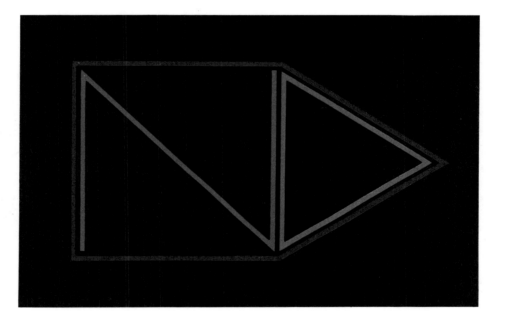

701

702

703

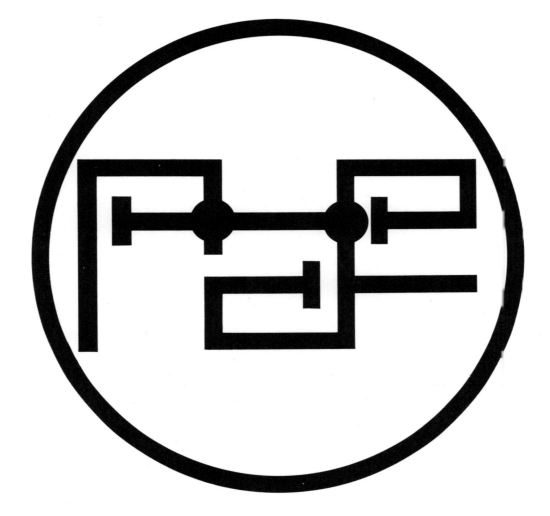

704

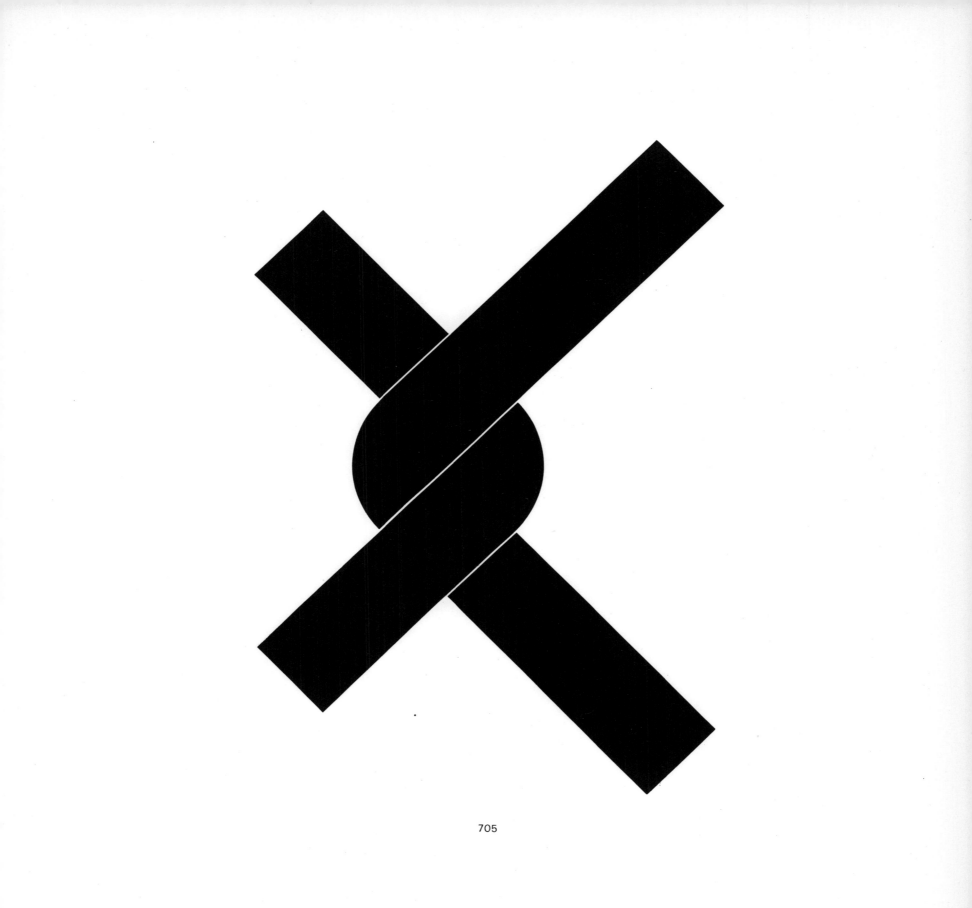

705

706

707

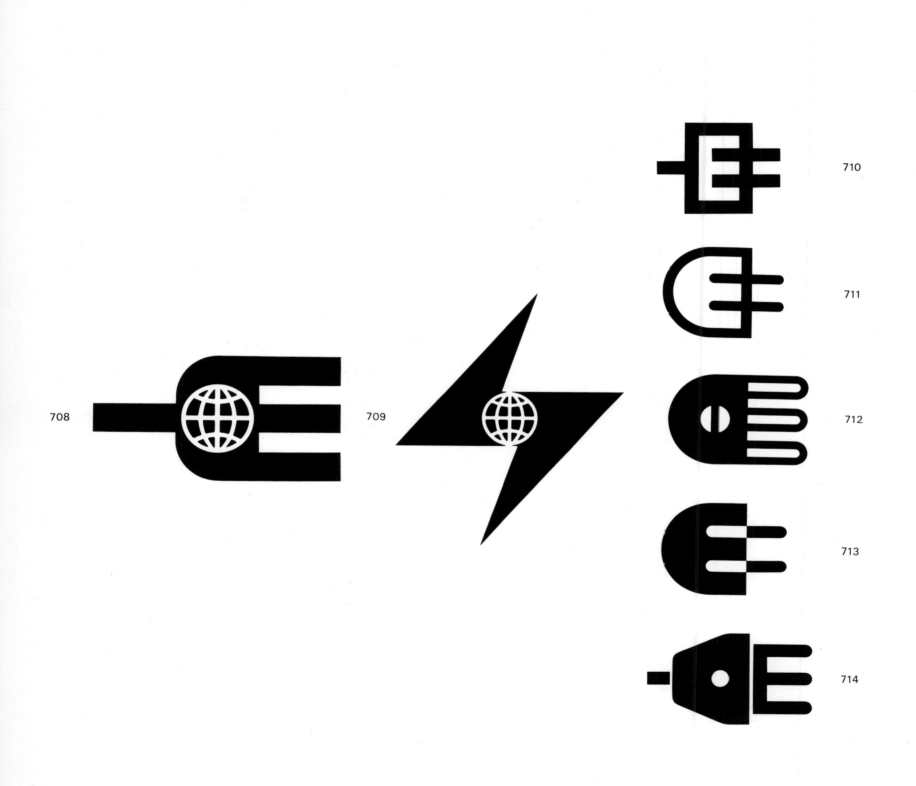

708

709

710

711

712

713

714

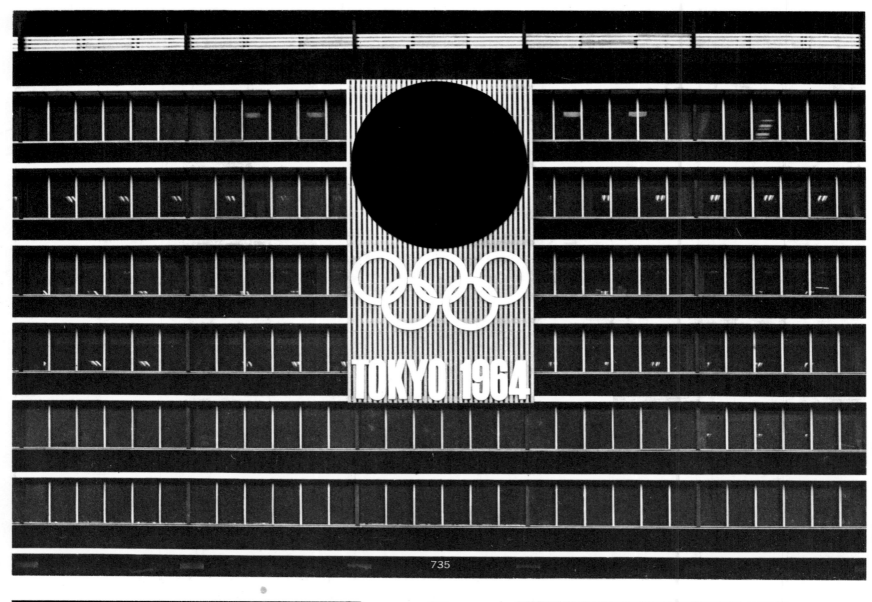

735

736

737

738

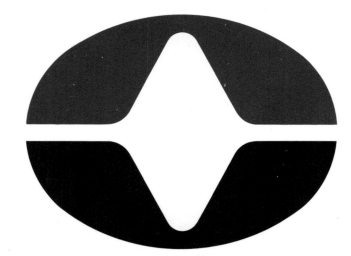

739

740

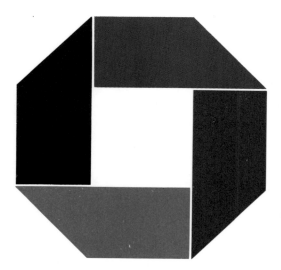

741

742

743

744

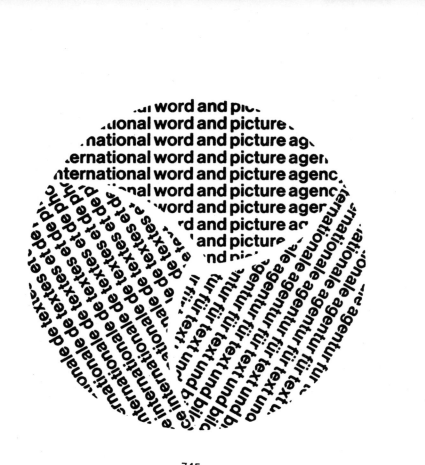

745

746

747

748

749

Immer mehr Baufirmen entscheiden
sich für Kistler-Schalungstafeln
mit Torstahlarmierung (patentiert).
Spezialverleimung und nach
Wunsch U-Schienen als Kanten-
schutz. Kistler-Schalungstafeln
sind heute in sechs verschiedenen
Ausführungen für jeden Zweck
und alle Ansprüche erhältlich.
Saubere Fugenbildung und schöne,
gleichmässige Struktur gewähr-
leisten bei sämtlichen Sichtbeton-
arbeiten hervorragende Resultate.

Wählen Sie das Bessere, wählen
Sie die meistgebrauchten Kistler-
Schalungstafeln.

Wir liefern auch rasch und zu-
verlässig Schal- und Gerüstholz zu
vorteilhaften Preisen. Dürfen wir
Ihre Anfrage erwarten?

Gottlieb Kistler & Söhne · Sägewerk / Schalungstafeln · Reichenburg / SZ Telefon 055 / 7 71 60

750

751

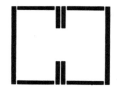

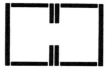

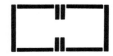

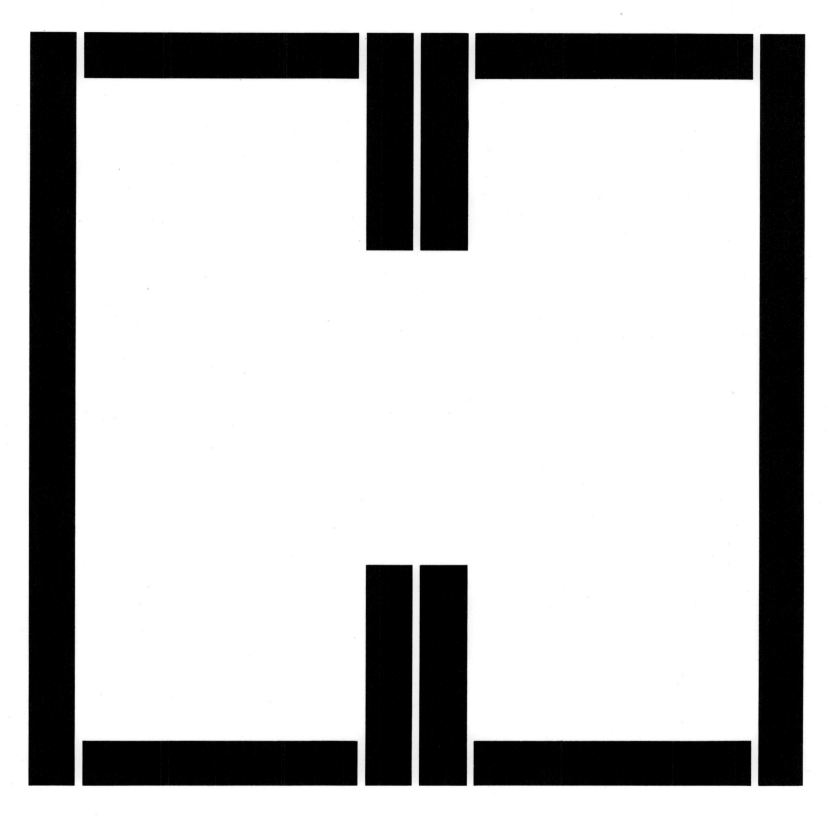

752

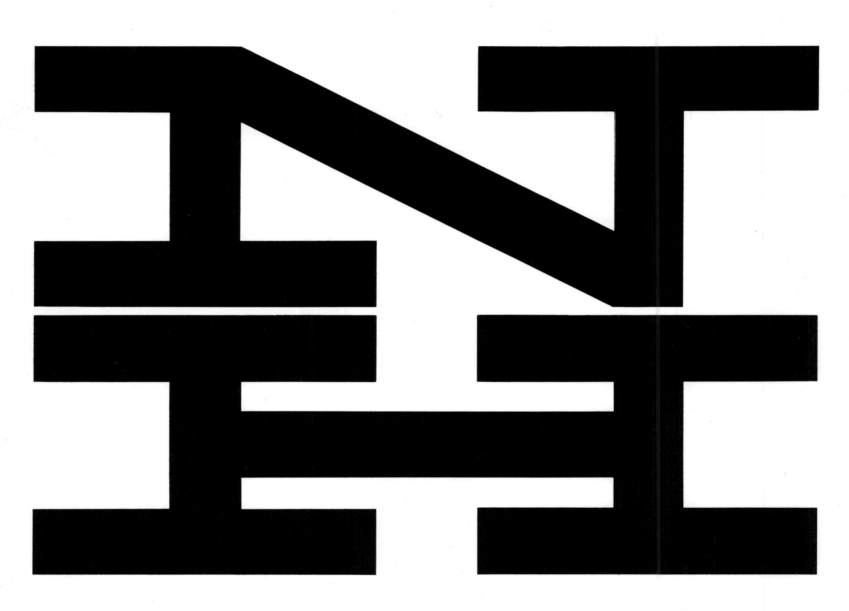

753

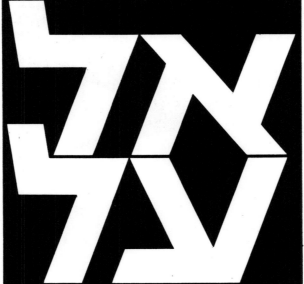

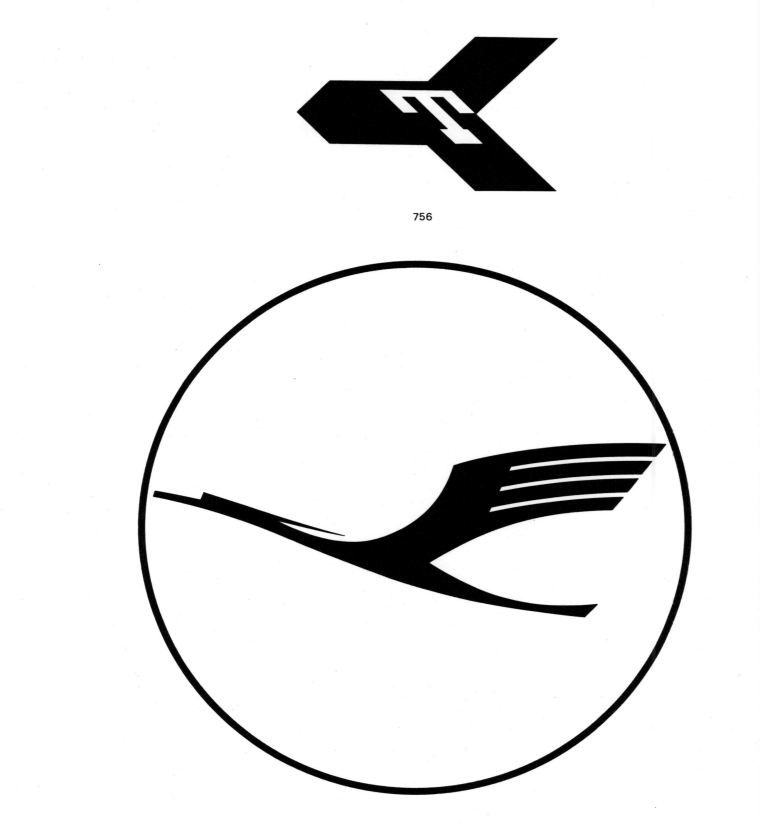

756

757

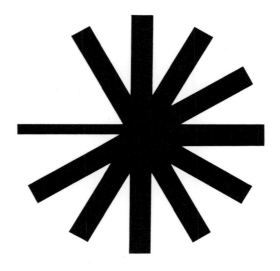

759

758

760

761

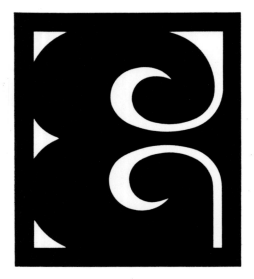

762

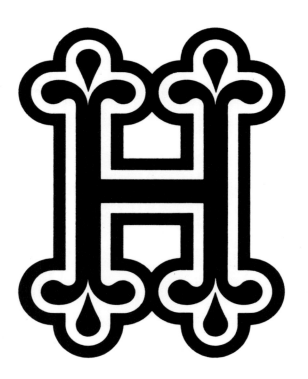

763

SOME NOTES ON TRADEMARK DESIGN

1

Practically all books published on trademarks start by describing their origin and history, then go on to provide examples classified according to one system or another, and end by discussing their use and effectiveness. Valid though this scheme may be, I have no intention of following it here.

I have prepared this book for designers and also for executives of companies and organizations who are responsible for selecting marks and symbols. It is possible that these executives may be more strongly impressed than designers by the unexpected world of symbols opening up before them in this book. Most people generally see trademarks or symbols standing alone and tend to think of them as unattractive, utilitarian things. In this book these isolated designs come together, at times seeming to interact like friends, or to complement one another, or to strike dramatic poses in unison.

It is the richness of themes and variations, and the lively vitality of the world of trademarks and symbols that I have attempted to show here—not only to designers and executives who commission symbols for their firms—but also to the general public to which the marks and symbols are directed.

It is common knowledge that in communicating with the public today, the mark or symbol makes an initial and important contribution. The corporate image starts with the mark, just as the laying of rails must be completed before the first train can run. Yet in regard to the trademarks, too many firms do not build upon the sound foundation needed to advance a favorable image.

Trademarks are an important means of guaranteeing product quality and of conveying the field of activity and scale of an enterprise. This is a fundamental principle in the creation of a corporate image.

" It is easier to remember a person's face than his name " is a statement often made in explaining the efficacy of trademarks. Most people do not pay attention outside their own sphere. How to impress a desirable image on this vast, indifferent public is a focal problem in present-day communications techniques.

In comparing the new trademarks and symbols sent to me from all over the world for this book with those in my earlier *Trademarks of the World* (New York, 1956), I must conclude that there has been no conspicuous progress in the intervening years. However, this is not surprising.

Trademarks and symbols always stretch the talent and capabilities of the designer to the utmost. Their creation involves a meeting at an extreme point of form and content. The conceptual ability of human beings to create such highly refined forms simply cannot be expected to show any major change in the span of ten years. Moreover, a long life span is demanded of trademarks and symbols. It would not do for them to look old-fashioned soon after they have been designed; they would then be more like vignettes for a weekly magazine rather than effective aids in creating an image of a firm or organization. Since a long life span is thus a basic prerequisite for a successful trademark, it should be no cause for concern that there are no basic differences in design concepts between this book and my previous one.

Yet this does not mean that there was no need to bring out this volume. As I mentioned previously, this book is an expression of my own feeling for design; it also represents a record of ten years as seen through marks and symbols. The compilation of an adequate record of the past is an essential step in the birth of something new.

In considering this book as a record of the past, the birth of a large number of new trademarks and symbols during these last ten years strikes me as a socio-economic phenomenon of considerable interest. It reflects the birth, or at least the rejuvenation, of a large number of firms and organizations. It is a phenomenon of much greater significance than the designing of huge quantities of posters and pamphlets; and mirrors what appears to be a much faster rate of change during this period than during the pre-war era. In compiling this volume, my attention has been drawn to a number of factors affecting this: a fierce economic competition; a great mass of new consumers who are quickly sated and always seeking new stimulants; a society ever more attuned to living in the present only, to stressing appearance more than content.

2

In *Seven Designers Look at Trademark Design* (published by Paul Theobald, 1952), there is an essay by Bernard Rudofsky entitled "Notes on Early Trademarks and Related Matters." It is the best discussion of the history of trademarks, and all later writings on this subject rely to a greater or lesser extent on this essay. It is perhaps unavoidable that most of the later works borrow only the historical, illustrative matter, and lack Rudofsky's great powers of philosophical insight. As I mentioned at the beginning, I see no need to discuss the history of trademarks here; I can do no better than to refer the reader to Rudofsky's essay on this subject.

However, I would like to call attention to the appearance of color in trademarks and symbols; this is a recent phenomenon. In principle, trademarks must be able to stand up

to reproduction solely in black and white, because of the economics of mass-production printing. On the other hand, there is no doubt that the addition of color to trademarks and symbols greatly enhances their power to attract attention. The concept of the corporate image demands not only expression in a unique form but also its definite association with one particular color or combination of colors. One firm wants to express its "personality" through a blue-red combination; another chooses green for its color motif, and wants all its trucks painted green. The addition of color to trademarks raises difficult economic problems, but its effectiveness and strong appeal cannot be denied. A good example is the General Dynamics mark designed by Eric Nitsche (see page 66, No. 120). Between the letters G and D, eight different colors are inserted. This color scheme is used on letterheads and all other business forms. This mark raises various questions; from an economical point of view, it may be argued that it constitutes an unnecessary expense. However, from a design point of view, it can be maintained that this is an ideal way of creating an image. Perhaps it can be said that the adoption of the designer's ideas was made possible only because a design-oriented firm like General Dynamics was involved. In any event, the design is a bold, handsome one with a powerful appeal.

Saul Bass is the creator of the new mark of the Aluminum Corporation of America (ALCOA; see page 180, No. 497), which uses a combination of blue and red. Unfortunately, in this book it was impossible to reproduce it in the desired colors, and it is printed in green and black. ALCOA's old mark, in use before Saul Bass designed the new one, was also expressed in blue and red. In other words, this blue-red color scheme, with a triangle as its theme, was the basic symbol of the firm. In creating the new mark, Saul Bass succeeded in breathing fresh, pulsating life into this basic design of ALCOA. It takes a designer with a highly developed social sense to accomplish this.

I am one of those designers who do not place much faith in color theories. I believe that just about the only objects in which color problems can be solved successfully on the basis of theory are traffic signs. Colors with originality and fresh, artistic qualities are outside the province of theory. They are the result of delicate waves of sensibility within a single human being. It is the intuitive color sense of an artist, seeking to find an expression of his genius, which moves us. Many years ago, when I was young and foolish, I tried to do color analyses of the pictures of Paul Klee. I painted the individual colors one by one on 20-centimeter paper squares, but Paul Klee was nowhere to be found. There were only blue, or red, or yellow squares of paper. I tried to force Klee's colors into a combination in my designs, but the sensual, yet fresh and airy impression of his pictures, was entirely missing.

The matter may be dismissed by describing my efforts as childish, yet something close to what I did is being taught by color theorists. I have mentioned this because if the color shades used in trademarks are too subtle, they present difficulties in reproduction. Multi-color printing has made great strides, and so has the reproduction of color photographs, through advances in both photographic materials and printing techniques. As a result, trademarks are often reproduced in color along with color illustrations in advertisements. However, trademarks just as colorful as the pictures in the advertisements will recede into inconspicuousness, a phenomenon known to all concerned with design and printing. The common sense solution is the frequent use of simple and clear two-color combinations, such as red and black, black and green, black and yellow. It may be argued that, if this is so, there is no need for the intuitive color sense of a gifted artist, and that elementary color theory will be sufficient. This might be so if the only thing involved was the lining up of small squares of colored paper horizontally or vertically. However, trademark design is the creation of forms of every conceivable shape. The proper matching of colors to these intricate forms calls for much more than mechanical application of color theory, and requires the talents of a gifted designer. There is a world of difference between the effect made by the right, "live" combination of two colors and a wrong, "dead" combination. Unless the two-color combination is dramatic, and forcefully strikes the viewer, it would be better to have the trademark or symbol in simple black and white.

Apart from the trademarks of commercial firms and the symbols of various organizations,

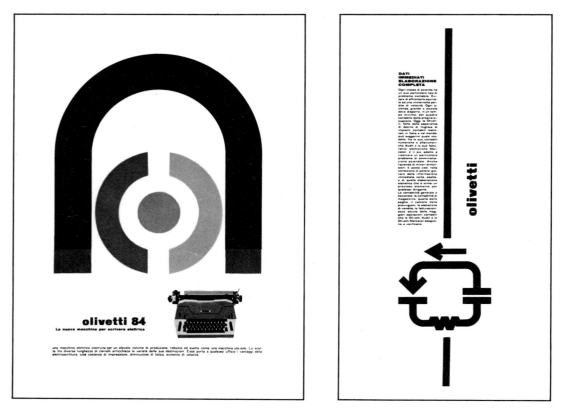

Examples of Olivetti advertisement applying symbols.

this book contains examples of what we might call signs or symbols used in advertising and product selling, such as the signs created by Giovanni Pintori for Olivetti products (Nos. 17, 33, 121, 137, 138, 139). They serve to impress upon the viewer the various calculating machines, typewriters, and other products produced by Olivetti, and are formed by the use of many colors. They play a star role in magazine advertisements and posters, and it is no exaggeration to say that they successfuly convey Olivetti's corporate image to the public. They are made up of clear, sharp colors. In this rare case, it might be said that the usual order of things has been reversed and that the individual gifts of the artist Pintori have shaped the characteristics of the Olivetti firm.

We see nothing strange in finger-prints being reproduced in black. But if those finger-prints are reproduced in red, they seem to reek of blood, and conjure up a scene of murder. Conversely, if a woman's lips are reproduced in black, it makes an eerie impression. We often hear of a woman sending her lover a letter ending with the red imprint of her lips. This is likely to stimulate the receiver sexually. But there are many different kinds of red. There is a sweet, romantic red, a dramatic, sexually exciting red, and others. It is said that the shape of every woman's lips is different, just as each person's finger-prints are unique. A woman's lips may thus be likened to her trademark, but the choice of lipstick color often expresses her character and breeding. The role of color in the corporate image is perhaps not unlike that of a woman's lipstick.

3

In my earlier book *Trademarks of the World*, I wrote:
"After a trademark has been selected, it must be tended. It must be kept fresh and alive. However, most businessmen become sentimentally attached to their

marks and are reluctant to change that which has seen them through many hardships as well as success. If these men stubbornly stick to the old and are unwilling to modify and modernize, their beloved symbols will no longer appeal to the public."

Ten years later, these words have not lost their validity; there are still many unenlightened entrepreneurs who try to run a streamlined train, namely their modernized production facilities, on the outworn rails of an old trademark. Admittedly, changing a trademark requires courage; it involves altering what has been promoted at great cost for many years. But the one who generally thinks that the expense has been worthwhile is the entrepreneur. I believe that trademarks require periodic hormone injections—that they should be changed little by little, in inconspicuous ways—to bring them into line with the taste of the period while still maintaining their excellence, and giving the general public a feeling of continuity.

An outstandingly successful example of this is the case of the Westinghouse trademark designed by Paul Rand. If the old mark and the present mark are compared, there is definite continuity in image, while the freshness of the new mark seems to be a revelation of the progressive character of the company. It deserves special mention that Westinghouse also had a new logotype designed at the same time as the company changed its mark. The success of Westinghouse in this area is the joint product of the talents of a great designer

Former mark.

Distinguishing features of the Westinghouse logotype; the ligature "st" and "g".

and the wisdom and decisiveness of the company's executives.

About three years ago I was consulted by a middle ranking Japanese pharmaceutical manufacturer about a change of trademark. This firm had used a "P" in a circle for about 80 years, and was interested in rejuvenating this mark. A competition for a new mark was held among four of Japan's representative designers. With the finished marks before us, I explained to the president of the company that there were two ways of effecting a change in a trademark—a radical change, and a gradual change, one step at a time. The first way meant doing away with the old mark completely without leaving a trace of its image, thus giving the impression that a new firm had come into existence. If the second method was followed, people other than specialists would scarcely notice the change, yet a vague impression

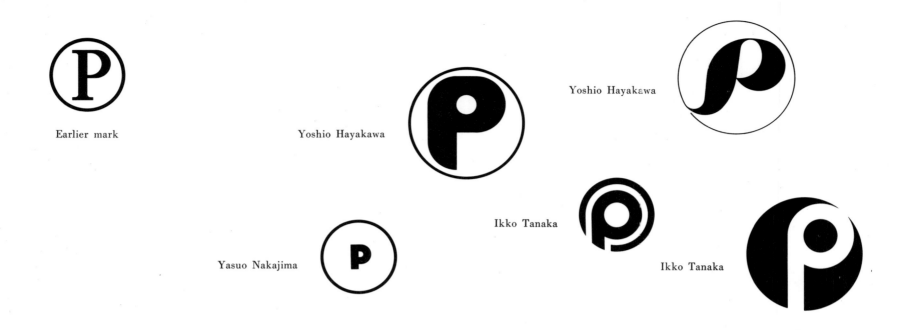

Earlier mark

Yoshio Hayakawa

Yoshio Hayakawa

Ikko Tanaka

Yasuo Nakajima

Ikko Tanaka

of rejuvenation would be conveyed. If the method of radical change was adopted everything else, such as newspaper advertisements, billboards, neon signs, and packages, would promptly have to be brought in line. This would involve enormous expense. With a one-step-at-a-time change, the process could be spread over a much longer period of time. The mark on boxes, for instance, could be changed when existing stocks were exhausted and a new printing ordered; billboards could be redesigned when physical replacement was necessary. I explained that the whole switch-over would take about two years and that it, of course, would cost much less than a radical change. In the end, the company decided to follow the one-step-at-a-time method.

I also pointed out it would be a mistake to think that the image of the company would become rejuvenated immediately just because of the new trademark. At the same time a new design policy would also have to be devised. So we also created a new logotype, and decided on a basic packaging design, in which, of course, the new trademark played a prominent part.

This case history is just one example from Japan; yet it shows the importance of using what may be called nothing more than ordinary common sense. Unfortunately this common

Selected new mark by Hiromu Hara

sense method is very seldom put into practice. Judging by my own experience, a company frequently commissions a new trademark from a designer, adopts it, and immediately feels that a distinct invigoration has taken place. But thereafter it does nothing to use the new trademark in a constructive and creative manner. No matter how much one may explain to the company executives what has to be done to utilize the new trademark fully, they do not listen. There are very few cases in which a company combines a new trademark with a new overall design policy, and thus really achieves successful results.

Outstanding examples of overall design planning are furnished by the works of Paul Rand for IBM (pages 22/23, Nos. 15, 16) and for Westinghouse (pages 120/121, Nos. 279, 280). The first step in drawing up an overall design policy is the creation of the trademark and of the logotype. Paul Rand's trademarks and logotypes (page 189, No. 560) possess a strength and beauty which transcend time, and thus have a very long life. They also have something which can be called "breadth." By this I mean that his marks fit in on any occasion and in any place. There are many interesting and appealing trademark designs: they may be chic, funny, lighthearted, or dramatic marks using new forms. However, their lack of breadth often becomes a problem. In other words, they are interesting and appealing but difficult to use.

They may not stand out when used on buildings; it may be impossible to make them into neon signs; they may not look good from a distance. Such marks all have the fault that only their original designers can use them to advantage. But marks and symbols must have sufficent breadth so that they come to life, whoever uses them. To come to life means that the mark or symbol does not interfere with other elements, but possesses the strength and beauty to harmonize with any surroundings.

4

A trademark or symbol must tell something about the purpose of the firm or organization it represents. This is a most elementary point to make about creating a corporate image, but one that cannot be overlooked. For example, it simply would not do if the marks of a chocolate manufacturer, a manufacturer of electrical appliances, and a steel works all conveyed a similar impression. In the mark of a chocolate manufacturer we want something of the sweetness and showiness of his products, while for a steel works mark we want an impression of weight and strength. It is not surprising that many airline marks take the form of birds, wings, or spears.—conveying the impression of flight.   Among the airlines of the world, nine use birds, four use wings, and another four use spears.   This clearly shows the intention of the designers to strive for a simplified and yet easily recognizable image.

When I visited Max Huber's studio in Milan in 1964, I noticed that he was creating a strange, somehow unstable, half circle, with the letters "Besana" skilfully and dramatically placed at the bottom.   I was interested in this unstable form and asked him about it.   He explained that this was the form of a candy with the name imprinted on it—that was known to practically every Italian.   The silhouette of the candy was being combined with the letters to make a very powerful trademark, to be put on everything, from wrapping paper to packages and trucks.   This is an example of a successful overall design policy followed by a medium-size enterprise.

Another example of an easily understood and well thought-out trademark is that of the modular furniture manufacturer Christian Holzäpfel K.G. (pages 232/233, Nos. 751, 752) in Basel, designed by Karl Gerstner in collaboration with Gredinger & Kutter.   This mark explains the concept of modular furniture brilliantly in very simple form. The letter "H" is designed in such a way as to give the impression of being an assembled unit; interestingly, it can be used side-ways either long and narrow, or short and squat.   These variations in no way damage the image of the trademark.   When it is used in magazine advertisements

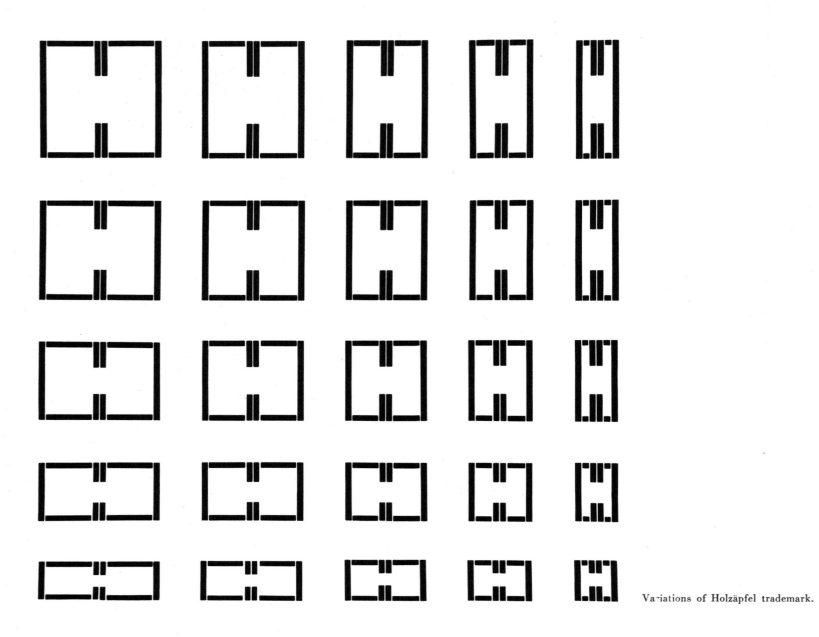

Variations of Holzäpfel trademark.

and pamphlets, the size of the mark is freely altered; however changed, it makes a strong impression on the viewer.

The trademark's function of clearly indicating the purpose of the enterprise is an important aid in sales. At the same time, it is highly desirable that the mark should also tell something about the size and nature of the enterprise for which it stands. It would not be appropriate for the marks of a one-man design office and a huge steel works, whose activity effects the economy of a whole country, to employ the same expression. Similarly, the trademark of a small store or workshop should not convey the same kind of impression as that of a huge electrical goods manufacturer. The mark should somehow express the scale and history of the enterprise, though this does not mean that it should have an antique air. What is neccessary is a suitable dignity.

Now let us assume that a good trademark has been chosen, and adopted by a company. The design is one that will make a strong, pleasant impression, and undoubtedly attract people. Unfortunately, such marks all too frequently end up in the president's desk drawer, or in the office safe, or only on stock certificates. A trademark exists to stamp itself indelibly upon the consciousness of the general public. This is the purpose of the corporate image. It must not be forgotten that a trademark has a strong psychological effect upon the general public. The image of a firm as huge, or outstanding, or progressive, or reliable owes much to the quality of the trademark design. Of course, the trademark by itself cannot create an image. Only where good design and overall design policy are combined, can a tiny mark in a corner of the product strongly convey the many facets of an image to the general public. Whether a trademark lives or dies depends on a careful and well thought-out design policy. Only if this exists, is it possible to deeply impress a corporate image on the general public.

ILLUSTRATION CREDITS

Note: Project indicates a design not in use at time of publication of this book.

11   1   Olle Eksell ⟨Sweden⟩   *Mazetti*.   Chocolate manufacturer.

12   2   Anton Stankowski ⟨Germany⟩   *Standard Elektrik Lorenz AG*.   Communications systems manufacturer.

13   3   George Giusti ⟨USA⟩   *Geigy*.   Chemical and pharmaceutical manufacturer.   Symbol for Hygroton.

14   4   Herb Lubalin, Inc. ⟨USA⟩   *Sudler, Hennessey & Lubalin*.   Design division of Sudler & Hennessey, Inc., advertising agency.

15   5   Saul Bass ⟨USA⟩   *Eastman Kodak Pavilion, New York World's Fair '64 -'65*.   The searching eye.

     6   Saul Bass ⟨USA⟩   *W.P. Fuller & Co*.   Paint manufacturer.

16   7   Charles Loupot ⟨France⟩   *Airline*.   (Project)

17   8   Morton Goldsholl Design Assoc. ⟨USA⟩   (Project)

18   9   Enzo Mari ⟨Italy⟩   *Danese*.   Ceramic and porcelain products manufacturer.   Package.

   10   Franco Meneguzzo ⟨Italy⟩   *Danese*.   Ceramic and porcelain products manufacturer.

19   11   Saul Bass ⟨USA⟩   *Lightcraft of California*.   Lighting fixtures manufacturer.

20   12   Sy Edelstein ⟨USA⟩   *King Solomon*.   Restaurant.

21   13   Robert R. Overby ⟨USA⟩   *Mitchell Travel Service*.   Travel agents.

   14   Rudolph de Harak ⟨USA⟩   *Ballard, Todd & Snibbe*.   Architects.

22   15-16   Paul Rand ⟨USA⟩   *International Business Machines Corp*.   Business machines manufacturer.   Packages and logotype.

24   17   Giovanni Pintori ⟨Italy⟩   *Olivetti*.   Symbol for Olivetti 48 typewriter.

25   18   Franco Grignani ⟨Italy⟩   *Maestrelli*.   Textile studies center.

   19   Max Huber ⟨Italy⟩   *Albitex*.   Cotton mill.

26	20	Richard Shiffer / George Nelson & Co., Inc. ⟨USA⟩ *Rek-o-Kut.* Audio equipment manufacturer.
	21	Collis Clements / Design Research Unit ⟨Great Britain⟩ *George Davidson & Co., Ltd.* Glass manufacturer.
	22	Yusaku Kamekura ⟨Japan⟩ *Taiyo Machine Industry Co.* Machine tools manufacturer.
	23	Ernst Roch ⟨Canada⟩ *Simtec Ltd.* Nuclear radiation detectors and monitors manufacturer.
27	24	Henrion Design Associates ⟨Great Britain⟩ *Brooks Ventilation Ltd.* Ventilation systems manufacturer.
28	25	Iris & Bruno Pippa ⟨Italy⟩ *Confezioni Coo.* Retail clothing store.
	26	Heinz Waibl ⟨Italy⟩ *Franco Ranchetti S.p.A.* Photocopying equipment manufacturer.
	27	Carl B. Graf ⟨Switzerland⟩ *Girsberger GmbH.* Furniture manufacturer.
	28	Nedo Mien Ferrario ⟨Venezuela⟩ *Galeria Esniral.* Art gallery.
	29	Allen, Dorsey & Hatfield ⟨USA⟩ *La Deau Manufacturing Co.* Symbol for Turnover Cradle, steel storage machine.
	30	Jerry Berman Associates ⟨USA⟩ *Nadisco Inc.* Tire inflator distributor.
	31	Anton Stankowski ⟨Germany⟩ Reproduction machinery manufacturer. (Project)
29	32	G. Soland + H. Schatzmann ⟨Switzerland⟩ *SAFFA.* Swiss exhibition of women's activities.
	33	Giovanni Pintori ⟨Italy⟩ *Olivetti.* Business machines manufacturer.
30	34	Saul Bass ⟨USA⟩ *"Exodus."* Motion picture.
31	35	Morton Goldsholl Design Associates ⟨USA⟩ *Butler Brothers.* Variety store chain. Private brands symbol.
	36	Saul Bass ⟨USA⟩ *SANE.* Committee for a Sane Nuclear Policy.
32	37	Rudolph de Harak ⟨USA⟩ *National Association of Radio & TV Broadcasters.* Trade association.
	38	Peter Graef ⟨USA⟩ *Castle & Cooke, Inc.* Food canners.
33	39	Gerd Leufert ⟨Venezuela⟩ *Venezuelan Pavillion, New York World's Fair '64 -'65.*
34	40	Percy Wenger ⟨Switzerland⟩ *Schweizerische Verpackungs Prämierung.* Swiss competition of packaging designs.
35	41	Frank Wagner ⟨USA⟩ *CBS Radio Network.* Symbol for a radio program.
36	42	Max Huber ⟨Italy⟩ *NAVA.* Printing company.
	43	Fred Witig / George Nelson & Co., Inc. ⟨USA⟩ *Structural Products Inc.* Aluminum products manufacturer.
	44	Wim Crouwel ⟨Netherlands⟩ *Nederlandse Kunsttichting.* Arts federation.
	45	Yusaku Kamekura ⟨Japan⟩ *Japan Photographers Society.*
	46	Lester Beall, Inc. ⟨USA⟩ *Merrill Lynch, Pierce, Fenner & Smith, Inc.* Stock brokers.
37	47-48	Paul Rand ⟨USA⟩ *Harcourt Brace & World, Inc.* Book publishers.

38	49	Max Huber ⟨Italy⟩ *22 Dicembre*. Movie productions.
	50	F.H.K. Henrion ⟨Great Britain⟩ *Layton Awards*. Competition for printing techniques.
	51	Bob Noorda ⟨Italy⟩. *La Rinascente / UPIM*. Department store chain. Quality control symbol.
	52	Max Huber ⟨Italy⟩ *Temi S.p.A.* Newspaper publisher and printer.
39	53	Max Huber ⟨Italy⟩ *Coin*. Department stores.
	54	Albe Steiner ⟨Italy⟩ *Foto Studio 22*. Photographers.
40	55	Hans Neuburg ⟨Switzerland⟩ *Plüss*. Printing company.
	56	G. Soland ⟨Switzerland⟩ *Union of Swiss Consumers Associations*. Co-operative food stores.
	57	Alfred Willimann ⟨Switzerland⟩ *Lignoplast A.G.* Interior decorators.
	58	Alfred Willimann ⟨Switzerland⟩ *Gromalto A.G.* Paint manufacturers.
41	59-61	Kurt Wirth ⟨Switzerland⟩ *Buri & Cie.* Printers.
42	62-64	Paul Rand ⟨USA⟩ *Atlas Crankshaft Corp.* Crankshafts manufacturer.
44	65	M. Schneider/Studio Boggeri ⟨Italy⟩ *Cantoni S.p.A.* Textile manufacturer.
	66	Motoi Shigenari ⟨Japan⟩ *Toyobo Textile Co.* Showroom symbol.
45	67	Eckstein-Stone, Inc. ⟨USA⟩ *Dusal instrument*. Scientific instruments manufacturer.
	68	Brownjohn & Chermayeff & Geismar ⟨USA⟩ *Malacandra Productions*. High fidelity recording firm.
	69	Hans Schleger ⟨Great Britain⟩ *Design Center*. Housemark.
	70	Rolf Harder ⟨Canada⟩ Venetian blinds manufacturer. (Project)
46	71	Push Pin Studios, Inc. ⟨USA⟩ *L'Escargot D'Or*. Restaurant.
	72	Morton Goldsholl Design Associates ⟨USA⟩ *Storkline Furniture*. Baby furniture manufacturer.
47	73	Erberto Carboni ⟨Italy⟩ *Ceramiques Laveno*. Ceramics manufacturer.
	74	Yusaku Kamekura ⟨Japan⟩ *Aburatsubo Yacht Club*.
	75	Arthur Paul ⟨USA⟩ *Playboy International*. Publisher, restaurateur, hotelier.
48	76	Neil Fujita ⟨USA⟩ *Record Source, Inc.* Publication.
	77	Appelbaum & Curtis ⟨USA⟩ *Richmond Research Corp.* Picture projectors manufacturer.
	78	Robert R. Overby ⟨USA⟩ *Mel Whitson Stationers, Inc.* Stationers.
49	79	Studio Boggeri ⟨Italy⟩ *Cantoni S.p.A.* Textile manufacturer.
	80	Klaus Winterhäger ⟨Germany⟩ C. *Feldmann*. Woodworking tools manufacturer.

49   81   Benno Wissing ⟨Netherlands⟩   *Aviso N.V.S.A.*   Building materials importer and wholesaler.

     82   F.H.K. Henrion ⟨Great Britain⟩   *Square Grip Reinforcement Co., Ltd.*   Reinforcing steel manufacturer.

50   83   Walter Allner ⟨USA⟩   *Fortune Films.*   Film producers.

51   84   Lippincott & Margulies, Inc. ⟨USA⟩   *United Van Lines, Inc.*   Transporters.

     85   Makoto Wada ⟨Japan⟩   *Mainichi Newspapers.*   Advertising design contest symbol.

     86   Walter Bosshardt ⟨Switzerland⟩   *Werner Noll.*   Optician.

     87   Morton Goldsholl Design Associates ⟨USA⟩   Advertising agency. (Project)

52   88   Ernst Roch ⟨Canada⟩   *Montreal International Fair.*

     89   M. Schneider/Studio Boggeri ⟨Italy⟩   *Cantoni S.p.A.*   Textile manufacturer.

53   90   Neil Fujita ⟨USA⟩   *Worldwide Broadcasting Company.*   Radio broadcasters.

     91   Erik Nitsche ⟨USA⟩   *Dorland, Inc.*   Advertising agency.

54   92   Everett S. Aison ⟨USA⟩   Film Pathways, Inc.   Motion picture producers.

     93   Leo Monahan ⟨USA⟩   *Eden Records.*   Popular records producer.

55   94   Saul Bass ⟨USA⟩   "*Anatomy of A Murder.*"   Motion picture.

56   95   Morton Goldsholl Design Associates ⟨USA⟩   *Munising Paper Co.*   Printing and typewriter paper manufacturer.

     96   Albe Steiner ⟨Italy⟩   *Libra.*   Book store.

57   97   Robert Geiber ⟨Switzerland⟩   *Krefina Bank A.G.*   Bank.

     98   Morton Goldsholl Design Associates ⟨USA⟩   *Peace Corps.*

58   99   Otl Aicher and Tomas Gonda ⟨Germany⟩   Oil trade company. (Project)

    100-101   Herbert Leupin ⟨Switzerland⟩   *Andre.*   Men's clothing store.

59   102   Ernst Roch ⟨Canada⟩   *Haas.*   Rope manufacturers.

    103   Peter Ray ⟨Great Britain⟩   *The Turks Head.*   Pub.

60   104   Push Pin Studios Inc. ⟨USA⟩   Own symbol.   Graphic designers.

    105   Hermann Eidenbenz ⟨Switzerland⟩   *Papyrus A.G.*   Stationers.

    106   Giulio Confalonieri ⟨Italy⟩   *Ditta Vergottini.*

61   107   Herb Lubalin Inc. ⟨USA⟩   Opening announcement of own design firm.

62   108   Theo Dimson ⟨Canada⟩   *Marlborough Hotel.*

    109   Herb Lubalin Inc. ⟨USA⟩   *Sand Grenade.*   Product for snow driving.

63 110 Theo Dimson ⟨Canada⟩ Printed matter for 12th Annual Award Ceremony of *Art Directors Club, Toronto.*

64 111 Max Bill ⟨Switzerland⟩ *Wohnbedarf A.G.* Homefurnishing manufacturer and retailer.

112 Alfred Willimann ⟨Switzerland⟩ *Karl Steiner.* Carpenters.

113 G. Soland ⟨Switzerland⟩ *Pendt A.G.* Shop builders.

114 Noel Martin ⟨USA⟩ *Westab.* Stationers and school supply manufacturer.

65 115 Heinz Waibl ⟨Italy⟩ *Allumino S.p.A.* Aluminum corporation.

116 Pierre Gauchat ⟨Switzerland⟩ *Riri Werke.* Zip fastener manufacturer.

117 Carlo Vivarelli ⟨Switzerland⟩ *Therma A.G.* Electrical appliances manufacturer.

118 Albe Steiner ⟨Italy⟩ *Ar-flex S.p.A.* Upholstered furniture manufacturer.

66 119 Don Ervin / George Nelson & Co., Inc. ⟨USA⟩ American National Exhibition in Moscow.

120 Erik Nitsche ⟨USA⟩ *General Dynamics Corp.* Defense systems manufacturer.

67 121 Giovanni Pintori ⟨Italy⟩ *Olivetti.* Business machines manufacturer.

68 122 Hans Neuburg ⟨Switzerland⟩ *Hyspa 1961.* Hygiene and sport exhibition.

123 Robert Sanbonet ⟨Italy⟩ *Triennale.* Design exhibition.

124 Carl B. Graf ⟨Switzerland⟩ *Kurth Certina Frères S.A.* Watch makers.

125 Kurt Wirth ⟨Switzerland⟩ *Chemische Fabrik Aarberg.* Printing colors manufacturer.

69 126 Kurt Wirth ⟨Switzerland⟩ *Swiss National Exhibition 1964.*

127 Lester Beall, Inc. ⟨USA⟩ *The Bunker-Ramo Corp.* Computer systems manufacturer.

128 Takashi Kono ⟨Japan⟩ *World Design Conference, Tokyo.*

129 Gustavo Balcells ⟨Argentina⟩ *Allende & Brea.* Patent agent.

130 Push Pin Studios, Inc. ⟨USA⟩ *Little, Brown & Co.* Book publishers.

131 Ove Engström ⟨Sweden⟩ *Bröderna Larsson.* Men's clothing manufacturer.

132 Alejandro Moy ⟨Argentina⟩ *The Argentine Chamber of Realtors.*

133 Otl Aicher ⟨Germany⟩ *Stuttgarter Gardinenfabrik.* Textile manufacturer.

134 A. Paez Torres ⟨Argentina⟩ *Fundacion Empresaizia.* Executives club.

135 Ernst Roch ⟨Canada⟩ *George F. Eber.* Architect.

136 Ernst Roch ⟨Canada⟩ *Artwood.* Office furniture manufacturer.

70 137-139 Giovanni Pintori ⟨Italy⟩ *Olivetti.* Symbol for electric computor.

71 140-141 Ladislav Sutnar ⟨USA⟩ *Carr's.* Department store.

72 142 Saul Bass ⟨USA⟩ *"The Cardinal."* Motion picture.

73 143 Morton Goldsholl Design Associates ⟨USA⟩ *International Minerals & Chemicals Corp.* Mineral and chemical manufacturer.

    144 Chris Yaneff + Manfred Gotthans ⟨Canada⟩ *United Dominions Corp.* Finance company.

74 145 Cecco Re ⟨Italy⟩ *A & B Insurance Brokers.*

    146 Cecco Re ⟨Italy⟩ *Impresi Turistiche Barziesi.* Tourist organization.

75 147 Heinz Waibl ⟨Italy⟩ *Termica.* Air conditioning machinery manufacturer.

    148 Heinz Waibl ⟨Italy⟩ *Pagina.* Graphic design magazine.

    149 Cecco Re ⟨Italy⟩ *Collana discografica IBC.* Record series.

76 150 Cecco Re ⟨Italy⟩ *Collana discografica IBC.* Record series.

    151 Gianni Venturino ⟨Italy⟩ *Calzificio Re Depaolini.* Hosiery store.

    152 Walter Ballmer ⟨Italy⟩ *Societa Italo Svizzera Fusioni Inettate.*

    153 Freeman Craw ⟨USA⟩ *CA.* Journal of commercial art.

    154 Lester Beall, Inc. ⟨USA⟩ *Martin Marietta Corp.* Electronic and nuclear manufacturers.

    155 Anton Stankowski ⟨Germany⟩ *Spinner.* Department store.

77 156 Takashi Kono ⟨Japan⟩ *Aji-no-moto.* Seasoning manufacturer.

    157 Takashi Kono ⟨Japan⟩ *Tombow Pencil Manufacturing Co.* Pencil symbol.

    158 Takashi Kono ⟨Japan⟩ *Miwa Pearl Co., Ltd.*

78 159 Karl Gerstner ⟨Switzerland⟩ *Arthur Niggli Verlag.* Book publisher.

    160 Hans Neuburg ⟨Switzerland⟩ *Eggler & Itschner.* Machine manufacturer for the paint industry.

    161 G. Honegger and G. Soland ⟨Switzerland⟩ *B.A.G. Turgi.* Lighting fixtures manufacturer.

    162 Heinz Waibl ⟨Italy⟩ *ENEL.* Electric Power Corporation.

79 163 Armin Hofmann ⟨Switzerland⟩ *Swiss National Fair, Lausanne 1964.*

    164 Noel Martin ⟨USA⟩ *Champion Paper Inc.* Paper manufacturer.

    165 Masayoshi Nakajo ⟨Japan⟩ *Asama Motor Lodge.*

    166 Keith Bright ⟨USA⟩ *Contact Products, Inc.* Pressure-sensitive paper manufacturer.

80 167 Ernst Roch ⟨Canada⟩ *Halifax Shopping Center.*

    168 Rose-Marie Joray ⟨Switzerland⟩ *Gottfried Pfenninger.* Electrical appliances.

80 169 Kenneth R. Hollick ⟨USA⟩ *Amosco.* Amalgated Asphalt Co. Ltd.

170 F.H.K. Henrion ⟨Great Britain⟩ *Simplex Concrete Piles Ltd.* Pile drivers.

171 R. Nelson, W. Bartch & Associates ⟨USA⟩ *George W. Barton & Associates.* Highway and traffic consultants.

172 Martti A. Mykkänen ⟨Finland⟩ *Asfaltor Oy.* Road constructors.

173 Jun Tabohashi ⟨Japan⟩ *Dentsu Driving Club.*

174 Martti A. Mykkänen ⟨Finland⟩ *Jalo Haapala & Co.* Construction company.

175 Jacques Nathan-Garamond ⟨France⟩ *Les Créations Graphiques.* Printers.

176 Gerd Leufert ⟨Venezuela⟩ *Ximenez Hnos.* Exporters-importers.

177 R.W. Mutch & Co. ⟨USA⟩ *Pockman Manufacturing Co.* Poultry coop wire and ventilating systems manufacturer.

178 Jun Tabohashi ⟨Japan⟩ *Prince Motor Sales Co. Ltd.* Car symbol.

81 179 Jacques Nathan-Garamond ⟨France⟩ *OECD.* Organization for Economic Expansion.

82 180 Tomoko Miho / George Nelson & Co., Inc. ⟨USA⟩ *Everbrite.* Electric signs manufacturer.

181 Erberto Carboni ⟨Italy⟩ *Exhibition: Italian Regions.*

83 182 Morton Goldsholl Design Associates ⟨USA⟩ *Miles Laboratories, Inc.* Pharmaceutical manufacturer. Symbol for Bactine skin cream.

183 Yusaku Kamekura ⟨Japan⟩ *Japanese National Commitee for World Power Conference.*

184 Rudolph de Harak ⟨USA⟩ *Cumberland Furniture Corp.* Furniture manufacturer.

185 Yusaku Kamekura ⟨Japan⟩ *Kinyo.* Textile wholesalers.

186 Albe Steiner ⟨Italy⟩ *Camadis S.p.A.*

84 187 George Him ⟨Great Britain⟩ *Australian Trade Commission.* Identification for Australian Sunshine Foods.

188 L. Sturne ⟨Italy⟩ *La Rinascente / UPIM.* Department store chain. Ceramic seal.

189 Bob Noorda ⟨Italy⟩ *La Comete.* Advertising agency for film and TV publicity.

190 Masayoshi Nakajo ⟨Japan⟩ *Ginza Shashin-Kosha.* Photography studio.

191 Ernst Roch ⟨Canada⟩ *Creative Photographers, Inc.* Photographic studio.

192 Marcel Wyss ⟨Switzerland⟩ *Roland von Siebenthal.* Potographers.

193 Anton Stankowski ⟨Germany⟩ Constructors. (Project)

194 Anton Stankowski ⟨Germany⟩ Constructors. (Project)

85 195 Anton Stankowski ⟨Germany⟩ Television signet for diaphragm and tower. (Project)

86 196 Helmut Lortz ⟨Germany⟩ *College of Fine Arts, Berlin.*

| 86 | 197 | Anton Stankowski ⟨Germany⟩ *Planen und Wohnen.* Furniture store. |

86 197 Anton Stankowski ⟨Germany⟩ *Planen und Wohnen.* Furniture store.

198 Ernst Roch ⟨Canada⟩ *Montreal Chamber Orchestra.*

199 Anton Stankowski ⟨Germany⟩ *Kornhaus.* Textile company.

87 200 Yusaku Kamekura ⟨Japan⟩ *Kenchiku-ka Kyokai.* Architects Association.

88 201 Yusaku Kamekura ⟨Japan⟩ *Yuken-boeki.* Mail order house.

202 Yusaku Kamekura ⟨Japan⟩ *Cultural exchange association.* (Project)

203 Yusaku Kamekura ⟨Japan⟩ *Daishowa Seishi.* Paper mills.

89 204 Morton Goldsholl Design Associates ⟨USA⟩ Electronics Company. (Project)

205 Don Ervin / George Nelson & Co., Inc. ⟨USA⟩ *Abbott Co.* Pharmaceuticals manufacturer.

90 206 Morton Goldsholl Design Associates ⟨USA⟩ Electronics company. (Project)

207 Morton Goldsholl Design Associates ⟨USA⟩ *Bauer & Black.* Elastic health garments manufacturer.

208 Morton Goldsholl Design Associates ⟨USA⟩ Vibrator and appliances manufacturer. (Project)

91 209 Morton Goldsholl Design Associates ⟨USA⟩ *Spencer Stuart & Associates.* Management consultants.

92 210 Max Huber ⟨Italy⟩ *Habitat.* Builders.

211 George Tscherny ⟨USA⟩ *Robert Zeidman Associates, Inc.* Industrial and package designers.

212 Jacques Nathan-Garamond ⟨France⟩ *Society of Industrial Arts.*

213 Walter Allner ⟨USA⟩ *Tri Inc.* Advertising Agency.

93 214 Takeshi Otaka ⟨Japan⟩ *Nada-man.* Restaurant.

215 Takeshi Otaka ⟨Japan⟩ *Hanataba.* Night club.

216 Takeshi Otaka ⟨Japan⟩ *Hitotsubu.* Restaurant.

217 Klaus Winterhäger ⟨Germany⟩ *Hans Winterhager, VDI.* Engineering office.

218 Michele Provinciali ⟨Italy⟩ *Poretti S.p.A.* Brewers.

94 219 Herb Lubalin Inc. ⟨USA⟩ *Eros Magazine, Inc.* Publication.

220 Herb Lubalin Inc. ⟨USA⟩ *Liaison Newsletter, Inc.* Publication.

95 221-222 Theo Dimson ⟨Canada⟩ *Harridge's.* Women's clothing store.

96 223 Push Pin Studios, Inc. ⟨USA⟩ *Franklin Simon.* Department store chain.

97 224 Helmut Lortz ⟨Germany⟩ Own symbol.

225 Romulo Maccio ⟨Argentina⟩ *Mirasol Libros.* Book publishers.

98 226 Aldo Calabresi / Studio Boggeri ⟨Italy⟩ *Tesom.* Men's clothing manufacturer.

227 Shigeo Fukuda ⟨Japan⟩ *Toyoko Department Store.* Symbol for merchandise series.

99 228 Hans Neuburg ⟨Switzerland⟩ + Anton Stankowski ⟨Germany⟩ *Sulzer AG.* Heavy machinery manufacturer.

229 Max Huber / Studio Boggeri ⟨Italy⟩ *Vitam.* Dried fruit company.

100 230 George Giusti ⟨USA⟩ *Doubleday & Co.* Book publishers. Symbol for American history series.

101 231 Arnold Schwartzmann ⟨Great Britain⟩ *Creative Partners Ltd.* Script-writers.

232 June Fraser / Design Research Unit ⟨Great Britain⟩ *Hodder Publications, Ltd.* Book publishers.

233 Goerge Giusti ⟨USA⟩ *Doubleday & Co.* Book publishers. Dolphin books series.

102 234 Giulio Confalonieri ⟨Italy⟩ *St. Andrews.* Restaurant.

235 Giulio Confalonieri ⟨Italy⟩ *Glencannon Whisky.*

236 Giulio Confalonieri ⟨Italy⟩ *The Whisky House.* Italian-English import firm.

103 237 Milner Gray / Design Research Unit ⟨Great Britain⟩ *Watney, Combe, Reid & Co., Ltd.* Brewers.

238 Kenneth Lamble and Collis Clements / Design Research Unit ⟨Great Britain⟩ *Dunlop Footwear Ltd.* Rubber footwear manufacturer.

104 239 Ronald Armstrong / Design Research Unit ⟨Great Britain⟩ *International Distillers and Vintners, Ltd.*

105 240 Giulio Confalonieri ⟨Italy⟩ Italian-English importers. (Project)

241 Ronald Armstrong / Design Research Unit ⟨Great Britain⟩ *Buisiness Equipment Trade Association.*

242 H.A. Rothholz & Associates ⟨Great Britain⟩ *Winsor & Newton Ltd.* Art supplies manufacturer.

243 Erik Ellegaard Frederiksen ⟨Denmark⟩ *SIG.* Swedish Association of Poster Designers.

106 244 Marcel Jacno ⟨France⟩ *Alhambra.* Music-hall.

245 Marcel Jacno ⟨France⟩ *Théâtre National Populaire.*

246 Morton Goldsholl Design Associates ⟨USA⟩ *Foulds Co.* Pasta manufacturer.

107 247 Jacques Nathan-Garamond ⟨France⟩ *OECD.* Organization for Economic Expansion.

248 June Fraser / Design Research Unit ⟨Great Britain⟩ *Finlay Shields.* Linen and towelling manufacturer.

108 249 Marco Del Corno ⟨Italy⟩ *Organizzazione Scuolo Nord.* School Organization.

250 Lello Castellaneta ⟨Italy⟩ *Balatum Italiana.* Tile manufacturer.

251 Helmuth Kurtz ⟨Switzerland⟩ *Evangelischer Verband Frauenhilfe.* Religious organization.

252 Ernst Roch ⟨Canada⟩ *Man and His World.* Canadian World Exhibition Corporation.

253 Keiko Hirohashi ⟨Japan⟩ *Meiji-Seimei.* Life insurance company.

108	254	Ernst Roch ⟨Canada⟩ *William S. Merrell Co.* Pharmaceutical manufacturer.
109	255	Rolf Harder ⟨Canada⟩ *Canadian Association for Retarded Children.*
110	256	Ernst Roch ⟨Canada⟩ *Riverside Housing.* Building Contractor.
	257	Yusaku Kamekura ⟨Japan⟩ *Nihon Prefab Jutaku.* Prefabricated housing manufacturer.
	258	Ernst Roch ⟨Canada⟩ *Smith Construction Corporation.* Building Contractor.
	259	Jean Picart Le Doux ⟨France⟩ *Fonderies de Pont-à-Mousson.* Foundries.
111	260	Milner Gray / Design Research Unit ⟨Great Britain⟩ *Building Center.*
	261	Lester Beall Inc. ⟨USA⟩ *International Paper Co.* Paper manufacturer.
112	262	Giulio Confalonieri ⟨Italy⟩ *Ditta Lerici Editori.* Publishers.
113	263	Celestino Piatti ⟨Switzerland⟩ *Artemis Verlag.* Publisher.
114	264	Bob Noorda ⟨Italy⟩ *Vallecchi Editore.* Publishers.
	265	Lars Bramberg ⟨Sweden⟩ *Nordiska Mässor.* Exhibition of Swedish cultural and industrial activities.
115	266-267	Lester Beall, Inc. ⟨USA⟩ *Hilton Hotel, New York.*
116	268	Saul Bass ⟨USA⟩ *Lawry's Food Products, Inc.* Spices and seasonings manufacturer.
	269	Lester Beall, Inc. ⟨USA⟩ *Titeflex, Inc.* Flexible tubing manufacturer.
	270	Saul Bass ⟨USA⟩ *Lawry's Food Products, Inc.* Spices and seasonings manufacturer.
117	271	Otl Aicher ⟨Germany⟩ *Steiger & Deschler.* Textile manufacturer.
	272	Theo Dimson ⟨Canada⟩ *William R. Rundle Ltd.* Importers.
	273	Bradbury Thompson ⟨USA⟩ *Society of Illustrators.*
	274	Olle Eksell ⟨Sweden⟩ *Nils Nessim.* Carpet store.
118	275	Morton Goldsholl Design Associates ⟨USA⟩ *Munising Paper Co.* Paper manufacturer.
	276	Eckstein-Stone, Inc. ⟨USA⟩ *H. &. K. Gross.* Textile manufacturer.
119	277	Morton Goldsholl Design Associates ⟨USA⟩ *Ditto Company, Inc.* Duplication products manufacturer. Package.
	278	Morton Goldsholl Design Associates ⟨USA⟩ *Ditto Company Inc.* Duplication products manufacturer.
120	279-280	Paul Rand ⟨USA⟩ *Westinghouse.* Electrical products manufacturer.(photo: Y. Ishimoto)
122	281	Gerd Leufert ⟨Venezuela⟩ *Pierre Denis.* Antique shop.
123	282	Yusaku Kamekura ⟨Japan⟩ *Takasaka Country Club.*
124	283	Jerry Braude ⟨USA⟩ *Boles-Aero Travel Trailer.* Transport company.

124 284 Rolf Harder ⟨Canada⟩ (Project)

285 Rolf Harder ⟨Canada⟩ Chicken farm. (Project)

286 Jan Hollender ⟨Poland⟩ *Pronit*. Record company.

287 Jan Hollender ⟨Poland⟩ *Slendaire*. Plastic surgery clinic.

288 Jerzy Cherka ⟨Poland⟩ *Iskry*. Publisher.

125 289 Stefan Bernacinski ⟨Czechoslovakia⟩ *Nasza Ksiegarnia*. Publisher.

290 Toni Burghart ⟨Germany⟩ *Täuber & Sohn*. Publisher.

291 Jiří Rathouský ⟨Czechoslovakia⟩ *Czechoslovak Airlines*.

292 Jiří Rathouský ⟨Czechoslovakia⟩ Artist's signet.

293 Fritjof Pedersen ⟨Sweden⟩ *Bonving Skofabrik*. Men's shoes manufacturer.

294 Seymour Augenbraum ⟨USA⟩ *Sterling Forest Gardens*. Park.

126 295 Saul Bass ⟨USA⟩ *The Trane Company*.* Ventilating systems manufacturer.

296 Saul Bass ⟨USA⟩ *Ivan Allen Company*.* Office supply retailers.

297 Theo Dimson ⟨Canada⟩ *Green, Blankstein & Russell, Ltd.* Architects.

298 Erik Nitsche ⟨USA⟩ Own letterhead.

127 299 Saul Bass ⟨USA⟩ *Samsonite*.* Luggage and folding furniture manufacturer. Luggage division.

300 Erik Nitsche ⟨USA⟩ *International Golf Association*.

301 George Tscherny ⟨USA⟩ *American Design Foundation*. Furniture manufacturer.

302 George Tscherny ⟨USA⟩ *Design Built Exhibits, Inc.* Exhibit and display builder.

128 303 Ralph Eckerstrom ⟨USA⟩ *Container Corporation of America*. Container manufacturer.

129 304 Kenji Ito ⟨Japan⟩ *Hotel Kirishima*.

305 Takashi Kono ⟨Japan⟩ *Daiwa Manekin Company*. Display models manufacturer.

130 306 Toshihiro Katayama ⟨Japan⟩ *Geigy*. Pharmaceutical manufacturer. Symbol for Hygroton.

307 George Giusti ⟨USA⟩ *Geigy*. Pharmaceutical manufacturer. Symbol for Preludin.

131 308 Saul Bass ⟨USA⟩. *Committee of Aluminum Producers*.

309 Matthew Leibowitz ⟨USA⟩ *Vector Manufacturing Co.* Electronic and aerospace instruments manufacturer.

132 310 Kurt Wirth ⟨Switzerland⟩ *Lithografie Zeiler AG*. Printer.

133 311 Giulio Confalonieri ⟨Italy⟩ *Ditta Lerici Editori*. Publisher.

*These are dummy letterheads (not in use) designed for a promotion booklet of sample letterheads for *Kimberly–Clark Corp.*, paper manufacturer.

134 312 Donald C. Smith ⟨USA⟩ *Art Directors & Designers' Association of New Orleans.*

313 Yusaku Kamekura ⟨Japan⟩ *Niigata-nippo.* Newspaper.

314 Augusto Concato ⟨Italy⟩ *Innocenti.* Automobile and machine manufacturer.

315 M. Schneider / Studio Boggeri ⟨Italy⟩ (Project)

135 316 Robert Berndt ⟨Germany⟩ Mail order house. (Project)

317 Lester Beall Inc. ⟨USA⟩ *Western Gypsum Products, Ltd.* Paint, plaster and cement manufacturer.

318 A. Ross and B. Thompson ⟨USA⟩ *Davis Delaney.* Printer.

136 319 Royal Dadman Associates ⟨USA⟩. *Diamond Alkali Co.* Chemical products manufacturer.

320 Gianni Venturino ⟨Italy⟩ *Rumianca S.p.A.* Chemical products manufacturer.

137 321 Paul Rand ⟨USA⟩ *United Parcel Service.* Parcel delivery company.

322 Pier Vico Cortesi ⟨Italy⟩ *Arti Grafiche Fantoni.* Graphic artists.

323 Wolfgang Freitag ⟨Germany⟩ Mail order house. (Project)

138 324 Ilio Negri ⟨Italy⟩ *Silkrom.*

325 Armin Hofmann ⟨Switzerland⟩ *Däniken.* Cable manufacturer.

326 Aldo Calabresi / Studio Boggeri ⟨Italy⟩ *Superga Industria Scarpe.* Shoe manufacturer.

327 Paul Rand ⟨USA⟩ *American Broadcasting Co.* Radio and TV network.

328 Ernst Roch ⟨Canada⟩ *Toilet Laundries Ltd.* Laundry and cleaning service.

329 Yusaku Kamekura ⟨Japan⟩ Japanese government seal of design approval.

330 Kohei Sugiura ⟨Japan⟩ *Tokyo Gallery.* Art gallery.

139 331 Albe Steiner ⟨Italy⟩ *Stagni.* Machinery manufacturer.

332 Hans Neuburg ⟨Switzerland⟩ *Ing. W. Oertli AG.* Oil heater manufacturer.

333 Jacques Richez ⟨Belgium⟩ *Brewery B.G.*

334 Jacques Richez ⟨Belgium⟩ *Atelier 3D.*

335 Allan R. Fleming + Jim Donahue ⟨Canada⟩ *Erin Mills Developments, Ltd.*

336 Judith Fralick ⟨Canada⟩ *MacDonald-Downie Ltd.* Printer.

140 337 Jacques Nathan-Garamond ⟨France⟩ *Plastugyl.* Plastic manufacturer.

338 Ikko Tanaka ⟨Japan⟩ *Toyota Motor Co., Ltd.* Symbol for the Publica automobile.

339 Jiří Rathousky ⟨Czechoslovakia⟩ Record edition.

140   340   Enzo Rösli 〈Switzerland〉 *Zip.* Match factory.

341   Marcel Wyss 〈Switzerland〉 *Rolf Jenni.* Musical instrument manufacturer.

342   Raymond Loewy Associates 〈France〉 *Nobel Bozel.* Chemical company.

343   R. Manson + v. Zuffellato 〈Italy〉 *Tito Piccoli Fotografo.* Photographers.

344   Kenji Ito 〈Japan〉 *Daido Interior Co., Ltd.* Decorators.

141   345   Jacques Nathan-Garamond 〈France〉 *Les Créations Graphiques.* Publisher.

346   Primo Angeli 〈USA〉 *Eastman Associates.* Public relations.

347   Mitsuo Katsui 〈Japan〉 *Sunayama Productions.* TV commercial films.

348   Wim Crouwel 〈Netherlands〉 *Municipal Museum van Abbe, Eindhoven.*

349   Yusaku Kamekura 〈Japan〉 *Dainippon Printing Ink & Chemical Co., Ltd.*

350   Otto Brunner 〈Germany〉 *Armaturenfabrik und Metallgiesserei.*

142   351   Chuck Rhoades 〈USA〉 *Continental Savings & Loan.* Bank.

352   Anton Stankowski 〈Germany〉 *Lufttechnische Gesellschaft.* Airconditioning and heating manufacturer.

353   Nedo Mien Feriario 〈Venezuela〉 *Banco Hipotecario de Credito Unido.* Bank.

354   Romulo Maccio 〈Italy〉 *Ediciones Mundonuevo.* Publisher.

355   Franco Grignani 〈Italy〉 Committee for Silk in Italy.

143   356   Anton Stankowski 〈Germany〉 *Lufttechnische Gesellschaft.* Airconditioning and heating manufacturer.

357   Muriel Cooper 〈USA〉 *M.I.T. Press.* Publishers.

358   Jacques Richez 〈Belgium〉 *Estro Armonico.* Club.

359   Carlo Vivarelli 〈Switzerland〉 *JWS.* Building machinery manufacturer.

360   Ladislav Sutnar 〈USA〉 *M-M Enclosures, Inc.* Metal containers manufacturer.

144   361   Herbert Auchli 〈Switzerland〉 Chemists.

362   Herbert Auchli 〈Switzerland〉 *Galvanite.* Galvanisers.

363   John Alcorn 〈USA〉 *Dutton Co.* Book Publishers. Everyman Paperback Series.

364   Gerard Douwe 〈Netherlands〉 *Netherlands Railways Ltd.*

365   Erberto Carboni 〈Italy〉 *Toninelli.* Art gallery.

366   Magalhaes + Noronha + Pontual 〈Brazil〉 *Brazilian Institute of Geography and Statistics.* Graphic service.

367   Nedo Mien Ferrario 〈Venezuela〉 *Harry A. Jarvis.* Personal monogram.

144	368	Nedo Mien Ferrario ⟨Venezuela⟩ *Arthur Proudfit.* Personal monogram.
	369	Max Huber / Studio Boggeri ⟨Italy⟩ *Scei.* Electric ovens manufacturer.
145	370	Erberto Carboni ⟨Italy⟩ *Radio Italiana.*
146	371	Walter Allner ⟨USA⟩ *Educational Broadcasting Corporation.*
	372	Irving Harper / George Nelson & Co., Inc. ⟨USA⟩ *Howard Miller Clock Co.* Clock and lamp manufacturer.
147	373	Paul Rand ⟨USA⟩ *Consolidated Cigar Corporation.*
	374	Allan R. Fleming ⟨Canada⟩ *Canadian National Railways.*
	375	Lester Beall Inc. ⟨USA⟩ *Connecticut General Life Insurance Company.*
148	376	Ray Engle ⟨USA⟩ *Noland Paper Company, Inc.*
	377	Everett S. Aison ⟨USA⟩ *Grossman Publishers, Inc.* Book publisher.
	378	Neil Fujita ⟨USA⟩ *Sixth Inter-America Accounting Conference.*
149	379-380	Herbert Leupin ⟨Switzerland⟩ *Panteen.* Hair conditioner. (380 is used more frequently than the simplified version, 379)
150	381	Theo Dimson ⟨Canada⟩ *Julie's.* Restaurant.
151	382	Erberto Carboni ⟨Italy⟩ *Bertolli.* Olive oil manufacturer.
	383	Marcel Jacno ⟨France⟩ *Gauloise.* Cigarettes.
	384	Piero Fornasetti ⟨Italy⟩ *Corisia.* Fabric house.
152	385	Anton Stankowski ⟨Germany⟩ Holding company. (Project)
	386	Vittorio Antinori Graphistudio ⟨Italy⟩ *La Caffetteria.* Coffee shop.
	387	Yusaku Kamekura ⟨Japan⟩ *Bunken-shuppan.* Publisher.
	388	Jaska Hänninen ⟨Finland⟩ *Boris Fehrmann.* Photographer.
	389	Giancarlo Guerrini ⟨Italy⟩ *Alessio Bassi.* Cutlery manufacturer.
	390	Heinz Waibl ⟨Italy⟩ *Radiotelevisione Italiana.* Quiz program symbol.
	391	Jerry Braude ⟨USA⟩ *Nancy Lee Martin.* Public Relations.
	392	Abram Games ⟨Great Britain⟩ *Inde Coope Ltd.* Brewer.
	393	Walter Baumberger ⟨Switzerland⟩ *Comité International de la Croix-Rouge.*
	394	Jerry Braude ⟨USA⟩ *Banner Printing Co.*
153	395	Christine & Ingo Friel ⟨Germany⟩ *Edeka.* Distillery of Gaston Cognac.
	396	Christine & Ingo Friel ⟨Germany⟩ *Baade & Endrulat.* Container manufacturer.

153 397 Erich Buchegger 〈Austria〉 *Vollhumon.* Fertilizer.

398 Ernst Roch 〈Canada〉 *Marquesa.* Knitwear manufacturer.

399 Karl Oskar Blase 〈Germany〉 (Project)

400 Yoshiro Yamashita 〈Japan〉 *Yomiuri-shuppan.* Book publisher. Symbol for series.

401 Marco Del Corno 〈Italy〉 *Cave Carbonate Calcio.* Chemical manufacturer.

402 Lester Beall Inc. 〈USA〉 *The East Ohio Gas Co.*

403 Benno Wissing 〈Netherlands〉 *Amsterdam Commission for Publicity of Books.*

154 404 Herbert Leupin 〈Switzerland〉 *Schweizerische Käseunion.* Swiss cheese manufacturers trade union.

155 405 Push Pin Studios, Inc. 〈USA〉 *Automatique.* Food vending machines manufacturer.

406 Morton Goldsholl Design Associates. 〈USA〉 *Holiday Delight Co.* Bakers.

156 407 Yusaku Kamekura 〈Japan〉 Children's wear manufacturer. (Project)

408 Francesco Saroglia 〈Italy〉 *International Wool Secretariat.* Wool mark of quality.

157 409 Gerard Wernars 〈Netherlands〉 *Ten Cate.* Organization of textile industries.

410 Olle Eksell 〈Sweden〉 *Svenska Yllehuset.* Wool fabric industry.

411 Romulo Maccio 〈Argentina〉 *Aniversario Argentina.*

412 Olle Eksell 〈Sweden〉 *Melka AB.* Clothing manufacturer.

413 Romulo Maccio 〈Argentina〉 *Muestras S.A.*

158 414 Karl Erik Lindgren 〈Sweden〉 *Svenska Missionsforbundets Union.* Missionary union.

415 W. Hergoröther 〈Italy〉 *Zanichelli.* Machinery manufacturer.

416 Celestino Piatti 〈Switzerland〉 *Otto Butzberger.* Metal window frames manufacturer.

159 417 Willi Sutter 〈Switzerland〉 Knitted goods factory.

418 Gilles Robert 〈France〉 *L'Administration de la voie maritime du St. Laurent.*

160 419 Otl Aicher 〈Germany〉 *Schlaginstrumentfabrik Johannes Link.* Musical instruments manufacturer.

420 Ernst Roch 〈Canada〉 *Ross-Ellis Ltd.* Printer and lithographer.

161 421 Helmut Lortz 〈Germany〉 *Novum.* Graphic design group.

422 Kurt Wirth 〈Switzerland〉 *Swiss Travel Bureau.*

423 Karl Gerstner 〈Switzerland〉 *Schwitter AG.* Printing block manufacturer.

424 Gerd Leufert 〈Venezuela〉 *Institute of Industrial Design, Caracas.*

162 425 Takeshi Otaka ⟨Japan⟩ *Wagen-Shuzo Co., Ltd.* Brewers.

426 Allan Jungbeck ⟨Sweden⟩ *AB Kvarnmaskiner.* Grain equipment manufacturer.

427 Bertil Anderson-Bertilson ⟨Sweden⟩ (Project)

428 Walter Ballmer ⟨Italy⟩ *Confezioni Caliumi.* Dressmaker.

429 Carl Regehr ⟨USA⟩ *The International Telephone and Telegraph Corp.*

430 Gerd Leufert ⟨Venezuela⟩ *Control Center.* Industrial power supply.

163 431 June Fraser/Design Research Unit ⟨Great Britain⟩ *Slinger.* Commercial photographers, typesetters, and rubber stamp makers.

432 Frank Wagner ⟨USA⟩ *Nuhold American Corp.* Water repellent manufacturer.

433 Gerd Leufert ⟨Venezuela⟩ *Norte Sur.* Travel agency.

434 Walter Ballmer ⟨Italy⟩ *Laboratori Cosmochimici.* Chemical works.

435 Gerd Leufert ⟨Venezuela⟩ Artificial flower manufacturer. (Project)

436 Bertil Anderson-Bertilson ⟨Sweden⟩ *Boda Glasbruk.* Glass works.

437 Heinz Waibl ⟨Italy⟩ *Ceteco.* Carbon paper.

438 Romulo Maccio ⟨Argentina⟩ *Medium Publicidad.* Advertising agency.

439 Gerd Leufert ⟨Venezuela⟩ *Japanese Film Festival.*

440 Wim Crouwel ⟨Netherlands⟩ *Omniscreen.* Silkscreen printers.

164 441 Yusaku Kamekura ⟨Japan⟩ Japanese Association for the Promotion of Science. (Project)

442 Bertil Anderson-Bertilson ⟨Sweden⟩ *Svenska Stalpressnings AB.* Steel press. (Project)

443 Tetsuo Katayama ⟨Japan⟩ *Turner Color Works.* Art supplies manufacturer.

444 Yusaku Kamekura ⟨Japan⟩ Symbol for automobile. (Project)

445 Kurt Wirth ⟨Switzerland⟩ Electrical appliances manufacturer. (Project)

165 446 Jacques Richez ⟨Belgium⟩ *Conserveries Globus.* Fish canneries.

447 Yusaku Kamekura ⟨Japan⟩ Symbol for automobile. (Project)

448 Tetsuo Katayama ⟨Japan⟩ *Asada Iron Works Co., Ltd.*

449 Ove Engström ⟨Sweden⟩ *Svea Band & Pappers AB.* Paper and printing company.

450 Jacque Nathan-Garamond ⟨France⟩ *Herbst et Cie.* High-fidelity manufacturer.

451 Ernst Roch ⟨Canada⟩ *Dominion Oilcloth & Linoleum Co., Ltd.* Floorcovering and oilcloth manufacturer.

166 452 Toshihiro Kayatama ⟨Japan⟩ Pharmaceutical manufacturer. (Project)

166　453　Piero Sonsoni ⟨Italy⟩　*Sagdos.*　Printer.

167　454-456　Toshihiro Kayatama ⟨Japan⟩　Pharmaceutical manufacturer.　(Project)

　　　457　Klaus Winterhäger ⟨Germany⟩　*Baumgarten Co.*　Gas and water works.

　　　458　Toshihiro Katayama ⟨Japan⟩　Pharmaceutical manufacturer.　(Project)

　　　459　Edger Kung ⟨Switzerland⟩　*Lucerne Boat Club.*

168　460　Walter Allner ⟨USA⟩　*Equitable Life Insurance Society of the United States.*

　　　461　Herb Lubalin ⟨USA⟩　*Studebaker Co.*　Symbol for the Lark automobile.

　　　462　Giulio Confalonieri ⟨Italy⟩　*Gallery St. George.*

　　　463　Max Bill ⟨Switzerland⟩　*Corso.*　Restaurant.

　　　464　Bradbury Thompson ⟨USA⟩　*Salomon Brothers & Hutzler.*　Stock brokers.

169　465　Saul Bass ⟨USA⟩　*Panaview Sliding Aluminum Door Company.*　Door manufacturer.

　　　466　Antonio Boggeri / Studio Boggeri ⟨Italy⟩　*Eston Confezioni.*　Men's clothing firm.

　　　467　George Tscherny ⟨USA⟩　*Chairmasters.*　Chair manufacturer.

　　　468　Robert Sidney Dickens ⟨USA⟩　*Packaging Corporation of America.*　Packaging products manufacturer.

　　　469　Heinz Waibl ⟨Italy⟩　*Symphonie.*　Foundation garments and bathing suit manufacturer.

170　470　Carlo Vivarelli ⟨Switzerland⟩　*Electrolux International.*　Electrical appliance manufacturer.

171　471　Anton Stankowski ⟨Germany⟩　Constructors.　(Project)

172　472　Neil Fujita ⟨USA⟩　*Pelican Films, Inc.*　Motion picture producers.

173　473　Richard P. Lohse ⟨Switzerland⟩　*Escher Wyss.*　Machine manufacturer.

174　474　Erberto Carboni ⟨Italy⟩　*Barilla.*　Pasta manufacturer.

175　475　Kurt Schwarz ⟨Austria⟩　*Kurt Steinwendner.*　Film producer.

176　476　Anton Stankowski ⟨Germany⟩　*Standard Electrik Lorenz Werke.*　Electrical products manufacturer.

　　　477　Ivan Chermayeff + Thomas Geismar ⟨USA⟩　*CIBA.* Information service of pharmaceutical company.

　　　478　Erich Buchegger ⟨Austria⟩　*Austro-Chematon.*　Scientific organization.

　　　479　Anton Stankowski ⟨Germany⟩　Real estate agent.　(Project)

177　480　Shigeo Fukuda ⟨Japan⟩　*Sankei Ad Monthly.*　Sankei Press.

　　　481　Max Huber ⟨Italy⟩　*Caprotti.*　Cotton mill.

178　482　Max Huber ⟨Italy⟩　*Casino Taormina.*　Restaurant and night club.

179 483 Frank Wagner ⟨USA⟩ (Project)

484 Yoshitaro Isaka + Keiko Takemura ⟨Japan⟩ *Toyo Rayon*. Product symbol.

485 Carl Brett ⟨Canada⟩ *Type House 1960*.

486 Elias Stieger ⟨Germany⟩ *Stieger Siebdruck Kaiserstuhl*. Printer.

487 M. Schneider / Studio Boggeri ⟨Italy⟩ *Studio per Industria Tessuti*. Textile studio.

488 Yusaku Kamekura ⟨Japan⟩ Mail order house. (Project)

489 Gerd Leufert ⟨Venezuela⟩ Lessons on Lithography by Leufert.

490 Yusaku Kamekura ⟨Japan⟩ *Taiyo Kikai-kogyo Co*. Machine manufacturer.

180 491 Tadashi Masuda ⟨Japan⟩ *Culleen*. Pencil manufacturer.

492 Takashi Kono ⟨Japan⟩ *Tokamachi Texile Association*.

493 Yusaku Kamekura ⟨Japan⟩ *Meguro Park Lane*. Bowling alley.

494 Gan Hosoya ⟨Japan⟩ *Asia Ski Manufacturing Company*. Ski manufacturer.

495 Luis Pals ⟨Germany⟩ Mail order house. (Project)

496 Giovanni Pintori ⟨Italy⟩ *Underwood*. Typewriter symbol.

497 Saul Bass ⟨USA⟩ *ALCOA*. Aluminum Company of America. Aluminum producer.

181 498 Bob Noorda ⟨Italy⟩ *Sonika*. Tape Recorder.

499 Kazumasa Nagai ⟨Japan⟩ *Kokusai Road Construction Corporation*.

500 Yusaku Kamekura ⟨Japan⟩ *Nihon Shinyaku*. Pharmaceutical manufacturer.

501 Takeshi Otaka ⟨Japan⟩ *Osaka Art Festival*.

502 Kenji Ito ⟨Japan⟩ *Canada Golf Shokai*. Golf goods manufacturer.

182 503 Koji Kato ⟨Japan⟩ *Sun Spice Inc*. Spices manufacturer.

504 Makoto Wada ⟨Japan⟩ *Light Publicity*. Design studio.

505 Kazumasa Nagai ⟨Japan⟩ *Nippon Research Center*. Market Research Company.

506 Gan Hosoya ⟨Japan⟩ *Kenchiku Mode Kenkyusho*. Architects.

507 Cecco Re ⟨Italy⟩ *Marketing Italia S.p.A*. Marketing office.

183 508 Kenji Ito ⟨Japan⟩ *Nippon Chromart Laboratory Inc*. Colour photography laboratory.

509 John Harrison ⟨Great Britain⟩ *Fisons Overseas Ltd*. Fertilizer and chemical manufacturer.

510 Leslie Smart + Sid Bersudsky ⟨Canada⟩ *Design Projects Center*.

183	511	Bob Noorda ⟨Italy⟩ *Metropolitana Milanese*. Milan underground railways.
	512	Heinz Waibl ⟨Italy⟩ *Officine Calabrese*. Truck factory.
	513	Jacques Nathan-Garamond ⟨France⟩ *Club Graphique*. Advertising Agency.
	514	Giulio Confalonieri ⟨Italy⟩ *Ditta Piriv*.
184	515	Rene Weiss ⟨Germany⟩ Mail order house. (Project)
	516	Shigeo Fukuda ⟨Japan⟩ *City Planning Promotion Movement*.
	517	Tadashi Masuda ⟨Japan⟩ *Endo Kenchiku Sekkei Jimusho*. Architects.
	518	Shigeo Fukuda ⟨Japan⟩ *Sanyo Electric Co., Ltd*.
	519	Dieter Einickt ⟨Germany⟩ Mail order house. (Project)
185	520	Makoto Wada ⟨Japan⟩ *Toyo Rayon*. Symbol for product Pylen.
	521	Otl Aicher ⟨Germany⟩ *Gral Glashuette*. Glasswares manufacturer.
	522	Hiram Ash / George Nelson & Co., Inc. ⟨USA⟩ *Scott Paper Co*. Paper products manufacturer.
	523	Unknown.
	524	Roy W. Madison ⟨USA⟩ *Stanrey Corp*. Pressed metal equipment manufacturer.
186	525	Louis Danziger ⟨USA⟩ *Sun-dormer International*. Sleep trailer manufactuerer.
	526	Nedo Mien Ferrario ⟨Venezuela⟩. *Lago Mar Beach*. Maracaibo nautical sports club.
	527	Charles McMurray ⟨USA⟩ *Stephens-Biondi-Decicco*. Aadvertising arts studio.
	528	Eranz Fässler ⟨Switzerland⟩ *Drawag*. Wire works.
	529	Magalhaes + Noronha + Pontual ⟨Brazil⟩ *Editore Delta SA*. Publisher.
	530	Bucher-Cremiéres ⟨France⟩ *Laboratoires Roland-Marie*.
	531	Franciszek Winiarski ⟨Poland⟩ Trade Union of Building Workers.
	532	Walter Ballmer ⟨Italy⟩ *Carema*. Wine.
	533	Gerard Wernars ⟨Netherlands⟩ *de Swaan-Bonnist*. Trading company.
	534	Nedo Mien Ferrario ⟨Venezuela⟩ *Ministerio de Agricultura y Cria*. Ministry of agriculture.
	535	F.H.K. Henrion ⟨Great Britain⟩ *Rapp Metals, Ltd*. Steel stockist.
	536	Joe Coroff / Promotion Design Associates ⟨USA⟩ *Film Projects Inc*. Film producers.
	537	Helmut Kurtz ⟨Germany⟩ *Apotheke Ehrensperger*. Druggist.
187	538	Edward P. Diehl ⟨USA⟩ *National Society of Art Directors, USA*.

187   539   Joseph Binder 〈Germany〉 *Öffentliche Bausparkassen Deutschlands*. Association of home finance banks.

540   Walter M. Kersing 〈Germany〉 *Sitos-Werke*. Baking powder manufacturer.

541   Jacques Nathan-Garamond 〈France〉 *Tourist Office, Düsseldorf*.

542   Ernst Roch 〈Canada〉 *CIBA*. Pharmaceutical manufacturer.

543   Stig Lindberg 〈Sweden〉 *AB Gustavsberg Fabriker*. Chinaware, plastic and enamel goods manufacturer.

544   Magalhaes + Noronha + Pontual 〈Brazil〉 *National Touristic Service*.

545   Eduart Ege 〈Germany〉 Official emblem of Munich.

546   Marcel Jacno 〈France〉 *René Julliart*. Publisher.

547   Romulo Maccio 〈Argentina〉 *Sudamericana*. Publisher. Symbol of series *Coleccion Teatro*.

548   Anton Stankowski 〈Germany〉 Fodder manufacturer. (Project)

549   Roger Geiser 〈Switzerland〉 *Joseph Diemand*. Sanitation engineers.

550   Per Einar Egger 〈Norway〉 *Shoe Export Norway*. Shoe exporters.

188   551   Hisami Kunitake 〈Japan〉 *Seven Foods Co., Ltd*. Food producers.

552   Gustavo Balcells 〈Argentina〉 *La Mercantil Rosarina*. Insurance company.

553   Klaus Winterhäger 〈Netherlands〉 *Geldermann & Zone*. Dutch textile manufacturer.

554   Heinz Waibl 〈Italy〉 *Societa Generale Semiconduttori*. Transistor and electronic component manufacturer.

555   Heinz Waibl 〈Italy〉 *Societa Electronucleare Nazionale*. Electronuclear company.

556   Aldo Calabresi / Studio Boggeri 〈Italy〉 *Pirelli*. Electrical appliance and rubber goods manufacturer.

557   Vance Jonson 〈USA〉 *E.M. Miller*.

558   Frank Wagner 〈USA〉 *Warner Chilcott Pharmaceutical Co*. Products symbol.

189   559   Kurt Schwartz 〈Austria〉 *Magnum*. German magazine.

560   Paul Rand 〈USA〉 *Westinghouse*. Electric appliances manufacturer.

561   Paul Rand 〈USA〉 *IIT Research Institute*.

562   Masayoshi Nakajo 〈Japan〉 *Nido Industrial Design Office*.

190   563-564   Freeman Craw 〈USA〉 *Tri-Art Press, Inc*. Printer.

565-566   Giulio Confalonieri 〈Italy〉 *Ditta Boffi*. Kitchenware manufacturer.

567   Rolf Harder 〈Canada〉 Trucking transporters. (Project)

191   568   F.H.K. Henrion 〈Great Britain〉 *Cox of Watford, Ltd*. Steel furniture manufacturer. Ash tray.

191   569   F.H.K. Henrion ⟨Great Britain⟩   *Cox of Watford, Ltd.*   Steel furniture manufacturer.

570   Theo Dimson ⟨Canada⟩   *Peterson Productions Ltd.*   Motion picture producers.

571   Lars Bramberg ⟨Sweden⟩   *Nordiska Mässor.*   Exhibition on roads and motoring.

192   572   Robert Pease ⟨USA⟩   *The Marin Jewish Community Center.*

193   573   Saul Bass ⟨USA⟩   "*Spartacus.*"   Motion picture.

574   Saul Bass ⟨USA⟩   "*Man with the Golden Arm.*"   Motion picture.

575   Saul Bass ⟨USA⟩   "*Advise and Consent.*"   Motion picture.

194   576   Milner Gray / Design Research Unit ⟨Great Britain⟩   *Board of Trade Council of Industrial Design.*

Rendering of Royal Coat of Arms.

577   Milner Gray / Design Research Unit ⟨Great Britain⟩   *Export Credits Guarantee Department.*

578   Milner Gray / Design Research Unit ⟨Great Britain⟩   *Ministry of Agriculture and Fisheries.*

579   Milner Gray / Design Research Unit ⟨Great Britain⟩   *P.&.O. Orient Lines.*   Steamship company.   Ship's badge for s.s. Oriana.

194   580-585   Milner Gray / Design Research Unit ⟨Great Britain⟩   *W. & A. Gilbey Ltd.*   Distillers and wine shippers.

Wyvern trademark.(various sizes and treatments to suit different puroposes)

195   586   Robert Perrit / Design Research Unit ⟨Great Britain⟩   *Westminster Wine Co.*   Wine and spirit retailer.

587   Milner Gray / Design Research Unit ⟨Great Britain⟩   *Austin Reed Ltd.*   Clothing manufacturer and retailer.

196   588   Hermann Eidenbenz ⟨Germany⟩   *Basel University.*   Diploma and seal of doctorate.

589   Celestino Piatti ⟨Switzerland⟩   *Kinderhilfe.*   Emblem for a fund providing school children with soap and milk.

590   Hermann Eidenbenz ⟨Germany⟩   *College of Music of Basel.*

197   591   Emil O. Biemann ⟨USA⟩   *United States Tobacco Co.*   Symbol for Sano cigarettes.

198   592   Piero Fornasetti ⟨Italy⟩   *Rizzi.*   Interiors and gift store.

593   Piero Fornasetti ⟨Italy⟩   *Ditta Fornasetti.*   Mark or trays.

594   Piero Fornasetti ⟨Italy⟩   *Ditta Fornasetti.*   Porcelain mark.

595   Piero Fornasetti ⟨Italy⟩   *Ditta Fornasetti.*   Porcelain mark.

596   Piero Fornasetti ⟨Italy⟩   *Ditta Fornasetti.*   Designer's mark.

597   Piero Fornasetti ⟨Italy⟩   *Ditta Fornasetti.*   Porcelain mark.

598   Piero Fornasetti ⟨Italy⟩   *Ditta Fornasetti.*   Porcelain mark.

599   Piero Fornasetti ⟨Italy⟩   *Ditta Fornasetti.*   Designer's mark.

199	600	Piero Fornasetti ⟨Italy⟩ *Ditta Fornasetti.* Porcelain mark.
	601	Piero Fornasetti ⟨Italy⟩ *Ditta Fornasetti.* Designer's mark.
	602	Piero Fornasetti ⟨Italy⟩ *Ditta Fornasetti.* Porcelain mark.
	603	Piero Fornasetti ⟨Italy⟩ *Ditta Fornasetti.* Porcelain mark.
	604	Piero Fornasetti ⟨Italy⟩ *Ditta Fornasetti.* Porcelain mark.
	605	Piero Fornasetti ⟨Italy⟩ *Ditta Fornasetti.* Porcelain mark.
	606	Piero Fornasetti ⟨Italy⟩ *Ditta Fornasetti.* Porcelain mark.
	607,608	Piero Foransetti ⟨Italy⟩ *Ditta Fornasetti.* Designer's marks.
200	609	Chwast + Glaser / Push Pin Studios, Inc. ⟨USA⟩ *Artone.* Artists' materials manufacturer. Studio India ink.
201	610	Verbena Rebora ⟨Italy⟩ *Ligure Lombarda.* Fruit preservers.
	611	Morton Goldsholl Design Associates ⟨USA⟩ Meat packers. (Project)
	612	Milner Gray ⟨Great Britain⟩ *Thomas de la Rue & Co., Ltd.* Banknote and security printer.
202	613	Fletcher + Forbes + Gill ⟨Great Britain⟩ *Goods & Chattels Ltd.* Fancy goods wholesalers.
203	614	Jane Sai ⟨USA⟩ *Hotel Sahara.*
204	615	Walter Allner ⟨USA⟩ *Reichhold Chemicals.* Chemical manufacturer.
205	616	Ernst Roch ⟨Canada⟩ Pulp and paper manufacturer. (Project)
	617	Stephan Lion ⟨USA⟩ *Hoffman La Roche, Inc.* Pharmaceutical manufacturer. Symbol for Posidron cough formula.
	618	C. Dradi ⟨Italy⟩ *Montecatini.* Chemical and mineral company.
	619	Wojciech Zamecnik ⟨Poland⟩ Chemical products.
	620	Kenji Ito ⟨Japan⟩ *Taiping Chemical Industry Ltd.* Chemical company.
	621	Albe Steiner ⟨Italy⟩ (Project)
206	622	Ladislav Sutnar ⟨USA⟩ *Golden Griffin.* Book publisher; book retailer.
	623	Nedo Mien Ferrario ⟨Venezuela⟩ *Cordon Bleu de Venezuela SA.* Food canners.
	624	John Massey ⟨USA⟩ *Chicago Pharmaceutical Co.* Pharmaceutical company.
	625	Giulio Confalonieri ⟨Italy⟩ *Galleria D'Arte Milano.* Art gallery.
	626	Rene Althaus ⟨Switzerland⟩ Ex Libris.
	627	Lane-Bender ⟨USA⟩ *Better Living Center, New York World's Fair '64-'65.*
	628	Giulio Confalonieri ⟨Italy⟩ *Ditta Impermeabili San Giorgio.* Rainwear manufacturer.

206   629 Flectcher + Forbes + Gill ⟨Great Britain⟩ *Percy Haynes & Co., Ltd.* Paper dealer.

630 Peter Beck ⟨Germany⟩ *Arbeitsgemeinschaft zur Eingliederung Behindter in die Volkswirtschaft.*

Association to promote the employment of the handicapped.

207   631 Helmuth Kurtz ⟨Switzerland⟩ (Project)

632 Masayoshi Nakajo ⟨Japan⟩ *Kushihara Shokai Co.* Leather tanners.

633 Ernst Roch ⟨Canada⟩ *Carl A. Donald Excavation Corp.* Excavator.

634 Rose-Marie Joray ⟨Switzerland⟩ *Interessengemeinscheft Reinen.* Local planning association.

635 Christine & Ingo Friel ⟨Germany⟩ *Studio Friel.* Graphic designers. (own symbol)

636 Jun Tabohashi ⟨Japan⟩ Symbol for silk fair.

637 Rolf Lagerson + Stig Bark ⟨Sweden⟩ *Gense.* Stainless steel works.

638 V. Antinori ⟨Italy⟩ *Amore e Pollastrini.* Canner.

639 Elfriede Anderegg ⟨Switzerland⟩ *CIBA.* Pharmaceutical manufacturer.

208   640 Keiko Hirohashi ⟨Japan⟩ *Yaesu Piano Co.*

641 Tomoko Miho / George Nelson & Co., Inc. ⟨USA⟩ *Creative Playthings, Inc.* Toy manufacturer. Learning center division.

642 Keiko Hirohashi ⟨Japan⟩ *Tokyo Star Lane.* Bowling alley.

643 F.H.K. Henrion ⟨Great Britain⟩ *Penguin Books Ltd.* Book publisher.

Symbol for Peacock Books, childrens' paperback book division.

644 Martti A. Mykkänen ⟨Finland⟩ *Uusikuvalehti.* Pictorial magazine.

209   645 Celestino Piatti ⟨Switzerland⟩ *Scheweizerische Zahnarzte Gesellschaft.* Anniversary meeting of a national dentists' association.

210   646-676 The Organizing Committee for the Games of the XVIII Olympiad, Tokyo. Signs indicating various facilities.

Designers; Masaru Katsumi, Ikko Tanaka, Yoshiro Yamashita, Keiko Hirohashi, Tadahito Nadamoto, Akira Uno,

Shigeo Fukuda, Wataru Ejima, Kuniomi Uematsu, Tadanori Yokoo, Tsunao Harada, Tsunehisa Kimura.

646 Official of the games.

647-652 (left to right): Woman Athlete, Man Athlete, Bath, Band, Shower, Post-Office.

653-658 (left to right): Lavatory, Club, Shopping Center, Sauna Bath, Ticket Office, Press Interview Room.

659-664 (left to right): Theater, Group Room, Dispensary, Clinic, Drinking Fountain, Dining Room.

665-670 (left to right): Telephone, Public Bus, Coat Room, Press Room, Lunch Room, Guest Room.

671-676 (left to right): Information, Locker Room, Bicycle Depot, Laundry, Olympic Village, Documentary Film.

212 677 Albe Steiner ⟨Italy⟩ *Teatro Popolare Italiano*.

678 Rolf Harder ⟨Canada⟩ Pharmaceuticals manufacturer. (Project)

679 Karl Erik Lindgren ⟨Sweden⟩ *Gumerssons Bokförlag*. Book publisher.

680 Hermann Virl ⟨Germany⟩ *Deutsche Bank*. Bank.

681 Magalhaes + Noronha + Pontual ⟨Brazil⟩ *Everon*. Photographic equipment manufacturer.

213 682 Anton Stankowsky ⟨Geramny⟩ *Friedrich Heyking*. Steel works.

683 Adolf Flückiger ⟨Switzerland⟩ *Tobacco Association of Switzerland*.

684 Armin Hofmann ⟨Switzerland⟩ *Pfauen*. Fasion center.

685 Rolf Harder ⟨Canada⟩ *Pharmacie Moderne*. Drug store chain.

686 Lester Beall, Inc. ⟨USA⟩ *Chance Vought Aircraft Inc*. Aircraft manufacturer.

214 687 Toshihiro Katayama ⟨Japan⟩ Pharmaceutical manufacturer. (Project)

215 688 Ikko Tanaka ⟨Japan⟩ *Kyodo Nyugyo Co*. Milk plant.

689 Klaus Winterhäger ⟨Germany⟩ *Firma Cürten*. Fishery.

216 690 Fletcher + Forbes + Gill ⟨Great Britain⟩ *International Scientific Systems*.

217 691 Morton Goldsholl Design Associates ⟨USA⟩ Electronics company. (Project)

692 Gerstner + Kuttner ⟨Switzerland⟩ *Swiss Watchmakers' Federation*.

693 Saul Bass ⟨USA⟩ *San Francisco International Film Festival*.

218 694 Franco Grignani ⟨Italy⟩ *Nereo Giroldi*. Reinforced concrete manufacturer.

695 Carlo Vivarelli ⟨Italy⟩ *Renggli*. Swiss interior decorators

696 Gerard Wernars ⟨Netherlands⟩ *Gevaert*. Film makers. Colored film symbol.

697 Morton Goldsholl Design Associates ⟨USA⟩ *Stone Container Corp*. Paperboard box manufacturer.

698 Olle Eksell ⟨Sweden⟩ *Landbrugets Avsaetningsudvalg*. Danish froozen food manufacturer.

219 699 Clifford Copeland ⟨Canada⟩ *The Canada Lithographing Co., Ltd*. Lithographer.

700 Fletcher + Forbes + Gill ⟨Great Britain⟩ *Anthony Blond*. Book publisher.

701 Kazumasa Nagai ⟨Japan⟩ *Nippon Design Center*.

702 Giulio Confalonieri ⟨Italy⟩ British-Italian import firm. (Project)

703 Armin Hofmann ⟨Switzerland⟩ *Mensch & Co*. Painters and plasterers.

220 704 Albe Steiner ⟨Italy⟩ *Pirelli*. Electrical appliances and rubber goods manufacturer.

221   705   Romek Marber ⟨Switzerland⟩ *Barnards*. Wire mesh manufacturer.

222   706   Fletcher + Forbes + Gill ⟨Great Britain⟩ *Designers & Art Directors Association*.

223   707   Chermayeff & Geismar Associates ⟨USA⟩ *United States Information Agency*. Symbol for exhibit "Graphic Arts U.S.A."

224   708-714   Competition of trademarks for *Electrolux International*.

      708   Ernest Witzig ⟨Switzerland⟩

      709   Ernest Witzig ⟨Switzerland⟩

      710   Marcel Wyss ⟨Switzerland⟩

      711   Hansruedi Widmer ⟨Switzerland⟩

      712   Otto Krämer ⟨Switzerland⟩

      713   Hansruedi Widmer ⟨Switzerland⟩

      714   Hans Wydler ⟨Switzerland⟩

225   715-734   Yoshiro Yamashita ⟨Japan⟩ Symbols indicating various games of Olympiad, Tokyo.

      (left to right): Track & Field, Rowing, Basketball, Boxing, Canoeing, Cycling, Fencing, Soccer, Gymnastics, Weight Lifting, Hockey, Judo, Wrestling, Swimming & Diving, Horsemanship, Shooting, Volleyball, Water Polo, Sailing.

226   735-736   Yusaku Kamekura ⟨Japan⟩ *Tokyo Olympiad*. Official symbol.

227   737   E. Mayerhofer ⟨Italy⟩ *Ombrasol*. Venetian blind manufacturer.

      738   Harold F. Walter ⟨USA⟩ *Chicago National Life Insurance Company*.

228   739   Lippincott + Margulies ⟨USA⟩ *Olin Mathieson*. Chemical company.

      740   Ivan Chermayeff + Gene Secander ⟨USA⟩ *Pepsi Cola*. Soft drink manufacturer.

      741   Chermayeff & Geismar Associates ⟨USA⟩ *The Chase Manhattan Bank*. Bank.

229   742   Ettore Sottsass ⟨Italy⟩ *Olivetti*. Business machines manufacturer.

      Symbol for Olivetti Elea 9003 Electronic computer.

230   743-744   Nelly Rudin ⟨Switzerland⟩ *Schwabenbräu A.G.* German brewer.

231   745   Gérard Ifert ⟨France⟩ *International Word & Picture Agency*.

      746   Fletchar + Forbes + Gill ⟨Great Britain⟩ *George Hoy*. Typographic designer.

      747   Ursula Hiestand ⟨Switzerland⟩ *Modissa AG*. Ladies' and childrens' wear manufacturer.

232   748   Siegfried Odermatt ⟨Switzerland⟩ *E.H. Schelling & Co.* Paperboard containers manufacturer.

      749-750   Siegfried Odermatt ⟨Switzerland⟩ *Gottlieb Kistler & Söhne*. Sawmill.

233　751-752　Gerstner + Gredinger + Kutter　〈Switzerland〉　*Christian Holzäpfel KG.*

234　753　Herbert Matter 〈USA〉　*New Haven and Hartford Railroad Company.*

235　754-755　Otto H. Treumann 〈USA〉　*EL AL Israel Airlines.*　Airline.

236　756　Yusaku Kamekura 〈Japan〉　*Tokyu Koku.*　Tourist agency.

　　757　Otto Firle 〈Germany〉　*Lufthansa.*　German airline. (Re-designed)

237　758　Michel Kin 〈France〉　*Mobilier International.*　Homefurnishings.

　　759　Kohei Sugiura + Kiyoshi Awazu 〈Japan〉　*The Japan Council Against A & H Bombs.*

　　760　Kazumasa Nagai 〈Japan〉　*Suruga Bank.*　Bank.

　　761　Thomas Laufer & Associates 〈USA〉　*San Francisco Seven.*　Designer's group.

238　762　Tom Daly + Peter Max 〈USA〉　*Daly & Max Ltd.*　Designer's own symbol.

　　763　Jerry Braude 〈USA〉　*Huntley Gaming Company.*　Game table manufacturer.

INDEX OF DESIGNERS

Numbers refer to illustrations

Aicher, Otl ⟨Germany⟩, 133, 271, 419, 521,
Aicher, Otl, and Tomas Gonda ⟨Germany⟩, 99
Aison, Everett S. ⟨USA⟩, 92, 377
Alcorn, John ⟨USA⟩, 363
Allen, Dorsey & Hatfield ⟨USA⟩, 29
Allner, Walter ⟨USA⟩, 83, 213, 371, 460, 615
Althaus, René ⟨Switzerland⟩, 626
Anderegg, Elfriede ⟨Switzerland⟩, 639
Anderson-Bertilson, Bertil ⟨Sweden⟩, 427, 436, 442
Angeli, Primo ⟨USA⟩, 346
Antinori, Vittorio/Graphistudio ⟨Italy⟩ 386, 638
Appelbaum & Curtis ⟨USA⟩, 77
Armstrong, Ronald/Design Research Unit ⟨Great Britain⟩, 239, 241
Ash, Hiram/George Nelson & Company, Inc. ⟨USA⟩, 522
Auchli, Herbert ⟨Switzerland⟩, 361–362
Augenbraum, Seymour ⟨USA⟩, 294
Awazu, Kiyoshi and Kohei Sugiura ⟨Japan⟩, 759

Balcells, Gustavo ⟨Argentina⟩, 129, 552
Ballmer, Walter ⟨Italy⟩, 152, 428, 434, 532
Bark, Stig, and Rolf Lagerson ⟨Sweden⟩, 637
Bartch, W. and Nelson, R. ⟨USA⟩, 171
Bass, Saul ⟨USA⟩, 5, 6, 11, 34, 36, 94, 142, 268, 270, 295–296, 299, 308, 465, 497, 573–575, 693
Baumberger, Walter ⟨Switzerland⟩, 393
Beall, Lester ⟨USA⟩, 46, 127, 154, 261, 266, 267, 269, 317, 375, 402, 686
Beck, Peter ⟨Germany⟩, 630
Berman, Jerry, Associates ⟨USA⟩, 30
Bernacinski, Stefan ⟨Czechoslovakia⟩, 289
Berndt, Robert ⟨Germany⟩, 316
Bersudsky, Sid, and Leslie Smart ⟨Canada⟩, 510
Biemann, Emil O. ⟨USA⟩, 591
Bill, Max ⟨Switzerland⟩, 111, 463
Binder, Joseph ⟨Germany⟩, 539
Boggeri, Studio, ⟨Italy⟩, 65, 79, 89, 226, 229, 315, 326, 466, 487, 523, 556
Blase, Karl Oskar ⟨Germany⟩, 399
Bosshardt, Walter ⟨Switzerland⟩, 86
Bramberg, Lars ⟨Sweden⟩, 265, 571
Braude, Jerry ⟨USA⟩, 283, 391, 394, 763
Brett, Carl ⟨Canada⟩, 485
Bright, Keith ⟨USA⟩, 166
Brownjohn, Chermayeff and Geismar ⟨USA⟩, 68
Brunner, Otto ⟨Germany⟩, 350
Bruno and Iris Pippa ⟨Italy⟩, 25
Buchegger, Erich ⟨Austria⟩, 397, 478
Bucher-Cremiéres ⟨France⟩, 530
Burghart, Toni ⟨Germany⟩, 290

Calabresi, Aldo/Studio Boggeri ⟨Italy⟩, 226, 326, 556
Carboni, Erberto ⟨Italy⟩, 73, 181, 365, 370, 382, 474

Castellaneta, Lello ⟨Italy⟩, 250
Cherka, Jerzy ⟨Poland⟩, 288
Chermayeff, Ivan and Thomas Geismar ⟨USA⟩, 477, 707, 741
Chermayeff and Geismar, Brownjohn and ⟨USA⟩, 68
Chermayeff, Ivan and Gene Secander ⟨USA⟩, 740
Chwast and Glaser/Push Pin Studios, Inc. ⟨USA⟩, 609
Clements, Collis/Design Research Unit ⟨Great Britain⟩, 21
Clements, Collis, and Kenneth Lamble/Design Research Unit ⟨Great Britain⟩, 238
Concato, Augusto ⟨Italy⟩ 314
Confalonieri, Giulio ⟨Italy⟩, 106, 234–236, 240, 262, 311, 462, 514, 565–566, 625, 628, 702
Cooper, Muriel ⟨USA⟩, 357
Copeland, Clifford ⟨Canada⟩, 699
Coroff, Joe/Promotion Design Associates ⟨USA⟩, 536
Cortesi, Pier Vico ⟨Italy⟩, 322
Craw, Freeman ⟨USA⟩, 153, 563–564
Crouwel, Wim ⟨Netherlands⟩, 44, 348, 440

Dadman, Royal, Associates ⟨USA⟩, 319
Daly, Tom and Peter Max ⟨USA⟩, 762
Danziger, Louis ⟨USA⟩, 525
de Harak, Rudolf ⟨USA⟩, 14, 37, 184
Del Corno, Marco ⟨Italy⟩, 249, 401
Design Research Unit ⟨Great Britain⟩, 21, 232, 237, 238, 241, 248, 260, 576–587
Dickens, Robert Sidney ⟨USA⟩, 468
Diehl, Edward P. ⟨USA⟩, 538
Dimson, Theo ⟨Canada⟩, 108, 110, 221–222, 272, 381, 570
Donahue, Jim and Allan R. Fleming ⟨Canada⟩, 335
Douwe, Gerard ⟨Netherlands⟩, 364
Dradi, C. ⟨Italy⟩, 618

Eckerstrom, Ralph ⟨USA⟩, 303
Eckstein-Stone, Inc. ⟨USA⟩, 67, 276
Edelstein, Sy ⟨USA⟩, 12
Ege, Eduart ⟨Germany⟩, 545
Eggen, Per Einar ⟨Norway⟩, 550
Eidenbenz, Hermann ⟨Switzerland⟩, 105, 588, 590
Einickt, Dieter ⟨Germany⟩, 519
Ejima, Wataru ⟨Japan⟩, 646–676 (see Illustration Credits)
Eksell, Olle ⟨Sweden⟩, 1, 274, 410, 412, 698
Engle, Ray ⟨USA⟩, 376
Engström, Ove ⟨Sweden⟩, 131, 449
Ervin, Don/George Nelson & Company, Inc. ⟨USA⟩, 119, 205

Fässler, Eranz ⟨Switzerland⟩, 528
Ferrario, Nedo Mien ⟨Venezuela⟩, 28, 353, 367–368 526, 534, 623
Firle, Otto ⟨Germany⟩, 757

Fleming, Allan R. ⟨Canada⟩, 374
Fleming, Allan R. and Jim Donahue ⟨Canada⟩, 335,
Fletcher/Forbes/Gill ⟨Great Britain⟩, 613, 629, 690, 700, 706, 746
Flückiger, Adolf ⟨Switzerland⟩, 683
Fornasetti, Piero ⟨Italy⟩, 384, 592–608
Fralick, Judith ⟨USA⟩, 336
Fraser, June/Design Research Unit ⟨Great Britain⟩, 232, 248, 431
Frederiksen, Erik Ellegaard ⟨Denmark⟩, 243
Freitag, Wolfgang ⟨Germany⟩, 323
Friel, Christine and Ingo ⟨Germany⟩, 395–396, 635
Fujita, Neil ⟨USA⟩, 76, 90, 378, 472
Fukuda, Shigeo ⟨Japan⟩, 227, 480, 516, 518, 646–676 (see Illustration Credits)

Games, Abram ⟨Great Britain⟩, 392
Geiber, Robert ⟨Switzerland⟩, 97
Geiser, Roger ⟨Switzerland⟩, 549
Geismar and Brownjohn and Chermayeff ⟨USA⟩, 68
Geismar, Thomas and Ivan Chermayeff ⟨USA⟩, 477, 707, 741
Gerstner, Karl ⟨Switzerland⟩, 159, 423, 692
Gerstner and Gredinger and Kutter ⟨Switzerland⟩, 751–752
Giusti, George ⟨USA⟩, 3, 230, 233, 307
Glaser and Chwast/Push Pin Studios, Inc. ⟨USA⟩, 609
Goldsholl, Morton, Associates ⟨USA⟩, 8, 35, 72, 87, 95, 98, 143, 182, 204, 206, 207–209, 246, 275, 277, 278, 406, 611, 691, 697
Gonda, Tomas and Otl Aicher ⟨Germany⟩, 99
Gotthans, Manfred and Chris Yaneff ⟨Canada⟩ 144
Graef, Peter ⟨USA⟩, 38
Graf, Carl B. ⟨Switzerland⟩, 27, 124
Gray, Milner/Design Research Unit ⟨Great Britain⟩, 237, 260, 576–585, 587, 612
Gredinger and Gerstner and Kutter ⟨Switzerland⟩, 751–752
Grignani, Franco ⟨Italy⟩, 18, 355, 694
Guerrini, Giancarlo ⟨Italy⟩, 389

Hänninen, Jaska ⟨Finland⟩, 388
Harada, Tsunao ⟨Japan⟩, 646–676 (see Illustration Credits)
Harder, Rolf ⟨Canada⟩, 70, 255, 284, 285, 567, 678, 685
Harper, Irving/George Nelson & Company, Inc. ⟨USA⟩, 372
Harrison, John ⟨Great Britain⟩, 509
Henrion, F.H.K., Design Associates ⟨Great Britain⟩, 24, 50, 82, 170, 535, 568–569, 643
Hergoröther, W. ⟨Italy⟩, 415
Hiestand, Ursula ⟨Switzerland⟩, 747
Him, George ⟨Great Britain⟩, 187
Hirohashi, Keiko ⟨Japan⟩, 253, 640, 642, 646–676

(see Illustration Credits)
Hofmann, Armin ⟨Switzerland⟩, 163, 325, 684, 703
Hollender, Jan ⟨USA⟩, 286, 287
Hollick, Kenneth R. ⟨Great Britain⟩, 169
Honegger, G. and C. Soland ⟨Switzerland⟩, 161
Hosoya, Gan ⟨Japan⟩, 494, 506
Huber, Max ⟨Italy⟩, 19, 42, 49, 52, 53, 210, 481, 482
Huber, Max/Studio Boggeri ⟨Italy⟩, 229, 369

Ifert, Gérard ⟨France⟩, 745
Ingo and Christine Friel ⟨Germany⟩ 395, 396, 635
Isaka, Yoshitaro and Keiko Takemura ⟨Japan⟩, 484
Ito, Kenji ⟨Japan⟩, 304, 344, 502, 508, 620

Janco, Marcel ⟨France⟩, 244, 245, 383, 546
Jonson, Vance ⟨USA⟩, 557
Joray, Rose-Marie ⟨Switzerland⟩, 168, 634
Jungbeck, Allan ⟨Sweden⟩ 426

Kamekura, Yusaku ⟨Japan⟩, 22, 45, 74, 183, 185, 200– 203, 257, 282, 313, 329, 349, 387, 407, 441, 444, 447, 488, 490, 493, 500, 735–736, 756
Katayama, Toshihiro ⟨Japan⟩, 306, 452, 454–456, 458, 687
Katayama, Tetsuo ⟨Japan⟩, 443, 448
Kato, Koji ⟨Japan⟩, 503
Katsui, Mitsuo ⟨Japan⟩, 347
Katsumi, Masaru ⟨Japan⟩, 646–676 (see Illustration Credits)
Kersing, Walter M. ⟨Germany⟩, 540
Krämer, Otto ⟨Switzerland⟩, 712
Kono, Takashi ⟨Japan⟩, 128, 156, 157, 158
Kutter and Gerstner and Gredinger ⟨Switzerland⟩, 751–752
Kimura, Tsunehisa ⟨Japan⟩, 646–676 (see Illustration Credits)
Kin, Michel ⟨France⟩, 758
Kung, Edger ⟨Switzerland⟩, 459
Kunitake, Hisami ⟨Japan⟩, 551
Kurtz, Helmut ⟨Switzerland⟩ 251, 537, 631

Lagerson, Rolf, and Stig Bark ⟨Sweden⟩ 637
Lamble, Kenneth, and Collis Clements/Design Research Unit ⟨Great Britain⟩, 238
Laufer, Thomas, & Associates ⟨USA⟩, 761
Lane-Bender ⟨USA⟩, 627
Leibowitz, Matthew ⟨USA⟩, 309
Leufert, Gerd ⟨Venezuela⟩, 39, 176, 281, 424, 430, 433, 435
Lindberg, Stig ⟨Sweden⟩, 543
Lindgren, Carl Erik ⟨Sweden⟩ 414, 679
Lion, Stephan ⟨USA⟩, 617
Lippincott & Margulies ⟨USA⟩, 84, 739
Loewy, Raymond, Associates ⟨France⟩, 342

Lohse, Richard P. ⟨Switzerland⟩, 473
Lortz, Helmut ⟨Germany⟩, 196, 224, 421
Loupot, Charles ⟨France⟩, 7
Lubalin, Herb, Inc. ⟨USA⟩, 4, 107, 109, 219, 220, 461
Leupin, Herbert ⟨Switzerland⟩, 100–101, 379–380, 404

Maccio, Romulo ⟨Argentina⟩, 225, 354, 411, 413, 438, 547
Madison, Roy W. ⟨USA⟩, 524
Magalhaes and Noronha and Pontual ⟨Brazil⟩ 366, 529, 544, 681
Manson, R. and v. Zuffellato ⟨Italy⟩, 343
Marber, Romek ⟨Switzerland⟩, 705
Mari, Enzo ⟨Italy⟩, 9
Martin, Noel ⟨USA⟩, 114, 164
Massey, John ⟨USA⟩, 624
Masuda, Tadashi ⟨Japan⟩, 491, 517
Matter, Herbert ⟨USA⟩, 753
McMurray, Charles ⟨USA⟩, 527
Meneguzzo, Franco ⟨Italy⟩, 10
Meyerhofer, E. ⟨Italy⟩, 737
Miho, Tomoko/George Nelson & Company, Inc. ⟨USA⟩, 180, 641
Monahan, Leo ⟨USA⟩, 93
Motoi, Shigenari ⟨Japan⟩, 66
Moy, Alejandro ⟨Argentina⟩, 132
Mutch, R.W., & Co. ⟨USA⟩, 177
Mykkänen, Martti A. ⟨Finland⟩, 174

Nadamoto, Tadahito ⟨Japan⟩, 646–676 (see Illustration Credits)
Nagai, Kazumasa ⟨Japan⟩, 499, 505, 701, 760
Nakajo, Masayoshi ⟨Japan⟩, 165, 190, 562, 632
Nathan-Garamond, Jacques ⟨France⟩, 175, 179, 212, 247, 337, 345, 450, 513, 541
Negri, Ilio ⟨Italy⟩, 324
Nelson, George, & Company, Inc. ⟨USA⟩, 20, 43, 119, 180, 205, 372, 522, 641
Nelson, R. and W. Bartch ⟨USA⟩, 171
Neuburg, Hans ⟨Switzerland⟩, 55, 122, 160, 332
Neuburg, Hans, and Anton Stankowski ⟨Switzerland⟩, 228
Nitsche, Erik ⟨USA⟩, 91, 120, 300
Noorda, Bob ⟨Italy⟩, 51, 189, 264, 498, 511

Odermatt, Siegfried ⟨Switzerland⟩, 748–750
Otaka, Takeshi ⟨Japan⟩, 214–216, 425, 501
Overby, Robert R. ⟨USA⟩, 13, 78

Pals, Luis ⟨Germany⟩, 495
Paul, Arthur ⟨USA⟩, 75
Pease, Robert ⟨USA⟩, 572
Pedersén, Fritjof ⟨Sweden⟩, 293
Perritt, Robert/Design Research Unit ⟨Great Britain⟩, 586

Piatti, Celestino ⟨Switzerland⟩, 263, 416, 589, 645
Picart le Doux, Jean ⟨France⟩, 259
Pintori, Giovanni ⟨Italy⟩, 17, 33, 121, 137–139, 496
Pippa, Iris and Bruno ⟨Italy⟩, 25
Promotion Design Associates ⟨USA⟩, 536
Provinciali, Michele ⟨Italy⟩, 218
Push Pin Studios, Inc. ⟨USA⟩, 71, 104, 130, 223, 405, 609

Rand, Paul ⟨USA⟩, 15–16, 47–48, 62–64, 279–280, 321, 327, 373, 560–561
Rathouský, Jiři ⟨Czechoslovakia⟩, 291–292, 339
Ray, Peter ⟨Great Britain⟩, 103
Re, Cecco ⟨Italy⟩, 145–146, 149, 150, 507
Rebora, Verbena ⟨Italy⟩, 610
Regehr, Carl ⟨USA⟩, 429
Rhoades, Chuck ⟨USA⟩, 351
Richez, Jacques ⟨Belgium⟩, 333–334, 358, 446
Robert, Gilles ⟨France⟩, 418
Roch, Ernst ⟨Canada⟩, 23, 88, 102, 135–136, 167, 191, 198, 252, 254, 256, 258, 328, 398, 420, 451, 542, 616, 633
Rösli, Enzo ⟨Switzerland⟩, 340
Ross, A. and Bradbury Thompson ⟨USA⟩, 318
Rotholz, H.A., & Associates ⟨Great Britain⟩, 242
Rudin, Nelly ⟨Switzerland⟩, 743–744

Sai, Jane ⟨USA⟩, 614
Sanbonet, Robert ⟨Italy⟩, 123
Sansoni, Piero ⟨Italy⟩, 453
Saroglia, Francesco ⟨Italy⟩, 408
Schatzmann, H. and G. Soland ⟨Switzerland⟩, 32
Schleger, Hans ⟨Great Britain⟩, 69
Schneider, M./Studio Boggeri ⟨Italy⟩, 65, 89, 315, 487
Schwartz, Kurt ⟨Austria⟩, 475, 559
Schwartzmann, Arnold ⟨Great Britain⟩, 231
Secander, Gene and Ivan Chermayeff ⟨USA⟩, 740
Shiffer, Richard/George Nelson & Company, Inc. ⟨USA⟩, 20
Skeehan, Maurice ⟨USA⟩, 92
Smart, Leslie and Sid Bersudsky ⟨Canada⟩, 510
Smith, Donald C. ⟨USA⟩, 312
Soland, G. ⟨Switzerland⟩, 56, 113
Soland, G., and G. Honegger ⟨Switzerland⟩, 161
Soland, G., and H. Schatzmann ⟨Switzerland⟩, 32
Sottsass, Ettore ⟨Italy⟩, 742
Stankowski, Anton ⟨Germany⟩, 2, 31, 155, 193–195, 197, 199, 352, 356, 385, 471, 476, 479, 548, 682
Stankowski, Anton, and H. Neuburg ⟨Germany⟩, 228
Stieger, Elias ⟨Germany⟩, 486
Steiner, Albe ⟨Italy⟩, 54, 96, 118, 186, 331, 621, 677, 704
Sturne, L. ⟨Italy⟩, 188
Sugiura, Kohei ⟨Japan⟩, 330
Sugiura, Kohei, and Kiyoshi Awazu ⟨Japan⟩, 759
Sutnar, Ladislav ⟨USA⟩, 140–141, 360, 622

Sutter, Willi ⟨Switzerland⟩, 417,

Tabohashi, Jun ⟨Japan⟩, 173, 178, 636
Takemura, Keiko and Yoshitaro Isaka ⟨Japan⟩, 484
Tanaka, Ikko ⟨Japan⟩, 338, 688, 646–676 (see Illustration Credits)
Thompson, Bradbury ⟨USA⟩, 273, 464
Thompson, Bradbury and A. Ross ⟨UAS⟩, 318
Torres, A. Paez ⟨Argentina⟩, 134
Treumann, Otto H. ⟨Netherlands⟩, 754–755
Tscherny, George ⟨USA⟩, 211, 301–302, 467

Uematsu, Kuniomi ⟨Japan⟩, 646–676 (see Illustration Credits)
Uno, Akira ⟨Japan⟩, 646–676 (see Illustration Credits)

Venturino, Gianni ⟨Italy⟩, 151, 320
Virl, Hermann ⟨Germany⟩, 680
Vivarelli, Carlo ⟨Switzerland⟩, 117, 359, 470, 695

Wada, Makoto ⟨Japan⟩, 85, 504, 520
Wagner, Frank ⟨USA⟩, 41, 432, 483, 558
Waibl, Heinz ⟨Italy⟩, 26, 115, 147–148, 162, 390, 437, 469, 512, 554–555
Walter, Harold F. ⟨USA⟩, 738
Weiss, Rene ⟨Germany⟩, 515
Wenger, Percy ⟨Switzerland⟩, 40
Wernars, Gerard ⟨Netherlands⟩, 409, 533, 696
Widmer, Hansruedi, ⟨Switzerland⟩ 711, 713
Willimann, Alfred ⟨Switzerland⟩, 57, 58, 112
Winiarski, Franciszek ⟨Poland⟩, 531
Winterhager, Klaus ⟨Germany⟩, 80, 217, 457, 553, 689
Wirth, Kurt ⟨Switzerland⟩, 59–61, 125–126, 310, 422, 445
Wissing, Benno ⟨Netherlands⟩, 81, 403
Witig, Fred/George Nelson & Company, Inc. ⟨USA⟩, 43
Witzig, Ernst,708–709
Wydler, Hans, ⟨Switzerland⟩ 714
Wyss, Marcel ⟨Switzerland⟩, 192, 341, 710

Yamashita, Yoshiro ⟨Japan⟩, 400, 715–734, 646–676 (see Illustration Credits)

Yaneff, Chris and Manfred Gotthans ⟨Canada⟩, 144
Yokoo, Tadanori ⟨Japan⟩, 646–676 (see Illustration Credits)

Zamecznik, Wojciech ⟨Poland⟩, 619
Zuffellato, v. and R. Manson ⟨Italy⟩, 343

INDEX OF CLIENTS

Numbers refer to illustrations

A & B Insurance Brokers, 145
Abbott Pharmaceuticals, 205
Aburatsubo Yacht Club, 74
L'Administration de la voie maritime du St. Laurent, 418
"Advise and Consent", 575
Aji-no-moto, 56
Albitex, 19
ALCOA, 497
Alessio Bassi, 389
Alhambra, 244
Allende & Brea, 129
Allumino Spa, 115
American Broadcasting Co., 327
American Design Foundation, 301
American National Exhibition, Moscow, 119
Amore e Pollastrini, 638
Amosco, 169
Amsterdam Commission for Publicity of Books, 403
"Anatomy of a Murder", 94
Andre, 100-101
Anniversario Argentina, 411
Apotheke Ehrensperger, 537
Arbeitsgemeinschaft zur Eingliederung Behindter in die Volkswirtschaft, 630
Ar-flex, SpA 118
Argentine Chamber of Realtors, 132
Armaturenfabrik und Metallgiesserei, 350
Art Directors and Designers Association of New Orleans, 312
Art Directors Club, Toronto, 110
Artemis Verlag, 263
Arti Grafiche Fantoni, 322
Artone, 609
Artwood, 135
Asada Iron Works Co., Ltd., 448
Asama Motor Lodge, 165
Asfaltor Oy, 172
Asia Ski Manufacturing, Co., 494
Atelier 3D, 234
Atlas Crankshaft Corp, 62—64
Austin Reed, Ltd., 587
Australian Trade Commission, 187
Austro-Chematon, 478
Aviso NVSA, 81

Baade & Endrulat, 396
Balatum Italiana, 250
Ballard, Todd & Snibbe, 14
Banco Hipotecario de Credito Unido, 353
Banner Printing Co., 394
Barilla, 474
Barnards, 705
Barton, George W., & Associates, 171

Basel University, 588
Bauer & Black, 207
Baumgarten Co., 457
Bertolli, 382
Better Living Center, New York World's Fair, 627
Blond, Anthony, 700
Board of Trade Council of Industrial Design, 576
Boda Glasbruk, 436
Boles-Aero Travel Trailer, 283
Bonving Skofabrik, 293
Brazilian Institute of Geography & Statistics, 366
Brewery BG, 333
Bröderna Larsen, 131
Brooks Ventilation, Ltd., 24
Building Center, 260
Bunken-shuppan, 387
Bunker-Ramo Corp, The, 127
Buri & Cie., 59—61
Business Equipment Trade Association, 241
Butler Brothers, 35
Butzberger, Otto, 416

CA (The Journal of Commercial Art), 153
Caffeteria, La, 386
Calzificio Re Depaolini, 151
Camadis SpA, 186
Canada Golf Shokai, 502
Canada Lithographing Co., Ltd., 699
Canadian Association for Retarded Children, 255
Canadian National Railways, 374
Canadian World Exhibition Corp., 252
Cantoni SpA, 79
Caprotti, 481
"Cardinal, The", 142
Carema, 532
Carr's, 140—141
Casino Taormina, 482
Castle & Cooke, Inc., 38
Cave Carbonato Calcio, 401
CBS Radio Network, 41
Ceramiques Laveno, 73
Certina, Kurt, Freres, SA, 124
Ceteco, 437
Chairmasters, 467
Champion Papers, Inc., 164
Chase Manhattan Bank, The, 741
Chemische Fabrik Aarberg, 125
Chicago National Life Insurance Company, 738
Chicago Pharmaceutical Co., 624
CIBA, 477, 542, 639
City Planning Promotion Movement, 516
Club Graphique, 513
Coin, 53
Collana Discografica IBC, 149, 150

Colleen, 491
College of Fine Arts, Berlin, 196
College of Music of Basel, 590
Comité International de la Croix-Rouge, 393
Committee of Aluminum Producers, 308
Committee for Silk in Italy, 355
Confezioni Calium, 428
Confezioni Coo, 25
Connecticut General Life Insurance Co., 375
Conserveries Globus, 446
Consolidated Cigar Corp, 373
Contact Products, Inc., 166
Container Corp. of America, 303
Continental Savings and Loan, 351
Control Center, 450
Coope, Inde, Ltd. 392
Cordon Bleu de Venezuela, 623
Corisia, 384
Corso, 463
Cox of Watford, Ltd., 568—569
Creations Graphiques, Les, 175, 345
Creative Partners, Ltd., 231
Creative Photographers, Inc., 191
Creative Playthings, Inc., 641
Cumberland Furniture, Corp., 184
Czechoslovak Airlines, 291

Daido Interior Co., Ltd., 344
Dainippon Printing Ink and Chemical Co., Ltd., 349
Daishowa Seishi, 230
Daiwa Manekin Co., 305
Daly and Max, Ltd., 762
Danese, 9, 10
Daniken, 325
Davidson, George, & Co, Ltd., 21
Delaney Davis, 318
Denis, Pierre, 281
Dentsu Driving Club, 173
Design Built Exhibits, Inc., 302
Design Center of Great Britain, 69
Design Projects Center, 510
Designers and Art Directors Association, 706
de Swaan-Bonnis, 533
Deutsche Bank, 680
Diamond Alkali Co., 319
Diemand, Joseph, 549
Ditta Boffi, 565—566
Ditta Fornasetti, 593—608
Ditta Lerici Editori, 262, 311
Ditta Piriv, 514
Ditta Vergottini, 106
Ditto Co., Inc., 277—278
Dominion Oilcloth & Linoleum Co., Ltd., 451
Donald, Carl. A. Excavation Corp., 633

Dorland, Inc., 91
Doubleday & Co., 230, 233
Drawag, 528
Dunlop Footwear, Ltd., 238
Dusal Instrument, 67
Dutton Co., 363

East Ohio Gas Co., The, 402
Eastman Associates, 346
Eastman-Kodak Pavillion, New York World's Fair, 5
Eber, George F., 135
Edeka, 395
Eden Records, 93
Ediciones Mundonuevo, 354
Editore Delta, SA, 529
Educational Broadcasting Corp., 371
Eggler & Itschner, 160
El Al Israel Airlines, 754—755
Electrolux AG, 445, 470, 708—714
Endo Kenchiku Sekkei Jimusho, 517
ENEL, 162
Equitable Life Insurance Society of the United States, 460
Erin Mills Developments Ltd., 335
Eros Magazine, Inc., 219
Escher Wyss, 473
Eston Confezioni, 466
Estro Armonico, 358
Evangelischer Verband Frauenhilfe, 251
Everbrite, 180
Everon, 681
Exhibition Italian Regions, 181
"Exodus", 34
Export Credits Guarantee Department, 577

Fehrmann, Boris, 388
Feldmann, C., 80
Film Pathways, Inc., 92
Film Projects, Inc., 536
Finlay Shields, 248
Firma Cürten, 689
Fisons Overseas Ltd., 509
Fonderies de Pont-à-Mousson, 259
Fortune Films, 83
Foto Studio 22, 54
Foulds Co., 246
Franklin Simon, 223
Fuller, W.P., & Co., 6
Fundacion Empresaizia, 134

Galeria Esniral, 28
Galleria D'Arte Milano, 625
Gallery St. George, 462
Galvanite, 362
Gauloise, 383

Gavaert Color Films, 696
Geigy, 3, 306, 307
Geldermann & Zone, 553
General Dynamics Corp., 120
Gense, 637
The Japan Council Against A & H Bombs, 759
Gibley, W. & A., Ltd., 580—585
Ginza Shashin-Kosha, 190
Girsberger GmbH, 27
Glencannon Whisky, 235
Golden Griffin, 622
Goods & Chattels, Ltd., 613
Gral Glashuette, 521
Green, Blankstein & Russell, Ltd., 297
Gromalto AG, 58
Gross, H. & K., 276
Grossman Publishers, Inc., 377
Gummersons Bokförlag, 679
Gustavsbergs Fabriker, AB, 543

Haapala, Jalo, & Co., 174
Haas, 102
Habitat, 210
Halifax Shopping Center, 167
Hanataba, 215
Harcourt Brace & World, Inc., 47—48
Harridge's, 221—222
Haynes, Percy, & Co., Ltd., 629
Herbst et Cie., 450
Hoy, George, 746
Heyking, Friedrich, 682
Hilton Hotel, New York, 266—267
Hitotsubu, 216
Hodder Publications, Ltd., 232
Hoffman La Roche, Inc., 617
Holiday Delight Co., 406
Holzapfel, Christian, KG, 751—752
Hotel Kirishima, 304
Hotel Sahara, 614
Huntley Gaming Co., 763
Hyspa 1961, 122

IIT Research Institute, 561
Impermeabili San Giorgio Ditta, 628
Impresi Turistiche Barziesi, 146
Innocenti, 314
Institute of Industrial Design, Caracas, 424
Interessengemeinschaft Reinen, 634
International Business Machines Corp., 15—16
International Distillers & Vintners, Ltd., 239
International Golf Association, 300
International Minerals & Chemicals Corp., 143
International Paper Co., 261
International Scientific Systems, 690

International Telephone & Telegraph Corp., The, 429
International Wool Secretariat, 408
International Word and Picture Agency, 745
Iskry, 288

Japan Photographers Society, 45
Japanese Film Festival, 439
Japanese Government Seal of Design Approval, 329
Japanese National Committee for World Power Conference, 183
Jarvis, Harry A., 367
Jenni, Rolf, 341
Julie's, 381
Julliart, Réne, 546
JWS, 359

Kenchiku-ka Kyokai, 200
Kimberley-Clark Corp., 295, 296, 299
Kinderhilfe, 589
King Solomon, 12
Kinyo, 185
Kistler, Gottlieb, & Söhne, 749—750
Kokusai Road Construction Corp., 499
Kornhaus, 199
Krefina Bank AG, 97
Kushihara Shokai Co., 632
Kvarnsmaskiner, AB, 426
Kyodo Nyugyo Co., 688

Laboratoires Roland-Marie, 530
Laboratori Cosmochimici, 434
La Comete, 189
La Deau Manufacturing Co., 29
Lago Mar Beach, 526
Landbrugets Avsaetningsudvalg, 698
La Rinascente/UPIM, 51, 188
Lawry's Food Products, Inc., 268, 270
Layton Awards, 50
L'Escargot d'Or, 71
Liaison Newsletter, Inc., 220
Libra, 96
Lightcraft of California, 11
Light Publicity, 504
Lignoplast AG, 57
Ligure Lombarda, 610
Lithografie Zeiler AG, 310
Little, Brown, & Co., 130
Lortz, Helmut, 224
Lubalin, Herb, Inc., 107
Lucerne Boat Club, 459
Lufthansa, 757
Lufttechnische Gesellschaft, 352, 356

MacDonald-Downie, Ltd., 336

Maestrelli, 18
Magnum, 559
Mainichi Newspapers, 85
Malacandra Productions, 68
Man and His World, 252
"Man with the Golden Arm", 574
Marin Jewish Community Center, The, 572
Marketing Italia SpA, 507
Marlborough Hotel, 108
Marquesa, 398
Martin Marietta Corp., 154
Martin, Nancy Lee, 391
Mazetti, 1
Medium Publicidad, 438
Meguro Park Lane, 493
Meiji-Seimei, 253
Melka AB, 412
Mensch & Co., 703
Mercantil Rosaria, La, 552
Merrell, William S., Co., 254
Merrill Lynch, Pierce, Fenner & Smith, 46
Metropolitana Milanese, 511
Miles Laboratories, Inc., 182
Miller, E.M., 557
Miller, Howard, Clock Co., 372
Ministerio de Agricultura y Cria, 534
Ministry of Agriculture & Fisheries, 578
Mirasol Libros, 225
Mitchell Travel Service, 13
M.I.T. Press, 357
Miwa Pearl Co., Ltd., 158
M-M Enclosures, Inc., 360
Mobilier International, 758
Modissa AG 747
Montecatini, 618
Montreal Chamber Orchestra, 198
Montreal International Fair, 88
Muestras SA, 413
Munich, 545
Municipal Museum van Abbe, 348
Munising Paper Co., 95, 275

Nada-man, 214
Nadisco, Inc., 30
Nasza Ksiegarnia, 289
National Association of Radio & TV Broadcasters, 37
National Society of Art Directors, USA, 538
National Touristic Service, 544
NAVA, 42
Nederlandse Kunsttichting, 44
Nereo Giroldi, 694
Nessim, Nils, 274
Netherlands Railways Ltd., 364
New Haven & Hartford Railroad Co., 753

Nido Industrial Design Office, 562
Niggli, Arthur, Verlag, 159
Nihon Prefab Jutaku, 257
Nihon Shinyaku, 500
Niigata-nippo, 313
Nippon Chromart Laboratory Inc., 508
Nippon Design Center, 701
Nippon Research Center, 505
Nitsche, Erik, 298
Nobel Bozel, 342
Noland Paper Co., Inc., 376
Noll, Werner, 86
Nordiska Mässor, 265, 571
Norte Sur, 433
Novum, 421
Nuhold American Corp., 432

OECD, 179, 247
Oertli, Ing. W., AG., 332
Offentliche Bausparkassen Deutschlands, 539
Officine Calabrese, 512
Olin Mathieson, 739
Olivetti 17, 33, 121, 137—139, 742
Olympiad XVIII, Organizing Committee for the Games
    of, 646—676, 715—734, 735—736
Ombrasol, 737
Omniscreen, 440
Organizzazione Scuolo Nord, 249
Osaka Art Festival, 501

P & O Orient Lines, 579
Packaging Corp. of America, 468
Pagina, 148
Panaview Sliding Aluminum Door Co., 465
Panteen, 379, 380
Papyrus AG, 105
Peace Corps, 98
Penguin Books, Ltd., 643
Pelican Films, Inc., 472
Pendt AG, 113
Pepsi Cola, 740
Peterson Productions Ltd., 570
PFAUEN, 684
Pfenninger, Gottfried, 168
Pharmacie Moderne, 685
Pirelli, 556, 704
Planen und Wohnen, 197
Plastugyl, 337
Playboy International, 75
Plüss, 55
Pockman Manufacturing Co., 177
Poretti SpA, 218
Prince Motor Sales Co., Ltd., 178
Pronit, 286

Proudfit, Arthur, 368
Push Pin Studios, Inc., 104
Pylen, 520

Radio Italiana, 370
Radiotelevisione Italiana, 390
Ranchetti, Franco, SpA, 26
Rapp Metals, Ltd., 535
Rathousky, Jiri, 292
Record Source, Inc., 76
Reichhold Chemicals, 615
Rek-O-Kut, 20
Renggli, 695
Richmond Research Corp., 77
Riri Werke, 116
Riverside Housing 256
Rizzi, 592
Ross-Ellis Ltd., 420
Rue, de la, Thomas, & Co., Ltd., 612
Rumianca SpA., 320
Rundle, William E., Ltd., 272

SAFFA, 32
Sagdos, 453
Salomon Brothers & Hutzler, 464
San Francisco International Film Festival, 693
San Francisco Seven, 761
Sand Grenade, 109
SANE, 36
Sankei Ad Monthly, 480
Sanyo Electric Co., Ltd., 518
Scei, 369
Schelling, E.H., & Co., 748
Schlaginstrumentfabrik Jahannes Link, 419
Schwabenbräu AG, 743—744
Schweizerische Zahnarzte Gesellschaft, 645
Schweizerische Käseunion, 404
Schweizerische Verpackungs Prämierung, 40
Schwitter AG, 423
Scott Paper Co., 522
Seven Foods Co. Ltd., 551
Shoe Export Norway, 550
Siebenthal, Roland von, 192
SIG, 243
Silk Fair, 636
Silkrom, 324
Simplex Concrete Piles, Ltd., 170
Simtec Ltd., 23
Sitos-Werke, 540
Sixth Inter-America Accounting Conference, 378
Slendaire, 287
Slinger, 431
Smith Construction Corp., 258
Societa Electronucleare Nazionale, 555

Societa Generale Semiconduttori, 554
Societa Italo Svizzera Fusioni Intettate, 152
Society of Illustrators, 273
Society of Industrial Arts, 212
Sonika, 498
"Spartacus," 573
Spencer Stuart & Associates, 209
Spinner, 155
Square Grip Reinforcement Co., Ltd., 82
St. Andrews, 234
Stagni, 331
Standard Elektrik Lorenz Werke, 476
Stanrey Corp., 524
Steiger & Deschler, 271
Steiger Siebdruck Kaiserstuhl, 486
Steiner, Karl, 112
Steinwendner, Kurt, 475
Stephens-Biondi-Decicco, 527
Sterling Forest Gardens, 294
Stone Container Corp., 697
Storkline Furniture, 72
Structural Products, Inc., 43
Studebaker Co., 461
Studio Friel, 635
Studio per Industria Tessuti, 487
Stuttgarter Gardinenfabrik, 133
Sudamericana, 547
Sudler, Hennessey & Lubalin, 4
Sulzer, 228
Sun Spice, Inc., 503
Sunayama Productions, 347
Sun-dormer International, 525
Superga Industria Scarpe, 326
Suruga Bank, 760
Svea Band & Pappers AB, 449
Svenska Missionforbundets Union, 414
Svenska Yllehuset, 410
Swiss Cheese Manufacturers Trade Union, 404
Swiss National Exhibition 1964, 126
Swiss National Fair, 163
Swiss Travel Bureau, 422
Swiss Watchmakers' Federation, 692
Symphonie, 469

Taiping Chemical Industry Ltd., 620
Taiyo Kikai-kogyo Co., 490
Taiyo Machine Industry Co., 22
Takasaka Country Club, 282
Täuber & Sohn, 290
Teatro Popolare Italiano, 677
Teni SpA, 52
Ten Cate, 409
Termica, 147
Tesom, 226

Théâtre National Populaire, 245
Therma, 117
Titeflex, Inc., 269
Tito Piccoli Fotografo, 343
Tobacco Association of Switzerland, 683
Toilet Laundries Ltd., 328
Tokamachi Textile Association, 492
Tokyo Gallery, 330
Tokyo Star Lane, 642
Tokyu Koku, 756
Toninelli, 365
Tourist Office, Düsseldorf, 541
Tombow Pencil Manufacturing Co., 157
Toyo Rayon, 484
Toyobo Textile Co., 66
Toyoko Department Store, 227
Toyota Motor Co., Ltd., 338
Trade Union of Building Workers, 531
Tri, Inc., 213
Tri-Arts Press Inc., 563—564
Triennale, 123
Turgi, BAG, 161
Turks Head, The, 103
Turner Color Works, 443
22 Dicembre, 49
Type House 1960, 485

Underwood, 496
Union of Swiss Consumers Associations, 56
United Dominions Corp., 144
United Parcel Service, 321
United States Tobacco Co., 591
United Van Lines Inc., 84
U.S.I.A., 707
Uusikuvalehti, 644

Vallecchi Editore, 264
Vector Manufacturing Co., 309
Venezuelan Pavillion, N.Y. World's Fair, 39
Vitam, 229
Vollhumon, 397
Vought, Chance, Aircraft, Inc., 686

Watney, Combe, Reid & Co., Ltd., 237
Westab, 114
Western Gypsum Products, Ltd., 317
Westminster Wine Co., 586
Westinghouse, 279—280, 560
Whisky House, The, 236
Whitson, Mel, Stationers, Inc., 78
Winsor & Newton, Ltd., 242
Winterhäger, Hans, VDI, 217
Wohnbedarf AG, 111
World Design Conference, 128

Worldwide Broadcasting Co., 90

Ximenez Hnos, 176

Yaesu Piano Co., 640
Yomiuri-shuppan, 400
Yuken-boeki, 201

Zanichelli, 415
Zeidman, Robert, Associates, Inc., 211
Zip, 340